PLAYWRITING, DRAMATURGY AND SPACE

Sara Freeman
University of Puget Sound

Shaftesbury Road, Cambridge CB2 8EA, United Kingdom

One Liberty Plaza, 20th Floor, New York, NY 10006, USA

477 Williamstown Road, Port Melbourne, VIC 3207, Australia

314–321, 3rd Floor, Plot 3, Splendor Forum, Jasola District Centre, New Delhi – 110025, India

103 Penang Road, #05–06/07, Visioncrest Commercial, Singapore 238467

Cambridge University Press is part of Cambridge University Press & Assessment, a department of the University of Cambridge.

We share the University's mission to contribute to society through the pursuit of education, learning and research at the highest international levels of excellence.

www.cambridge.org
Information on this title: www.cambridge.org/9781009467940

DOI: 10.1017/9781009370257

First published 2023

A catalogue record for this publication is available from the British Library

ISBN 978-1-009-46794-0 Hardback
ISBN 978-1-009-37022-6 Paperback
ISSN 2753-2798 (online)
ISSN 2753-278X (print)

Playwriting, Dramaturgy and Space

Elements in Contemporary Performance Texts

DOI: 10.1017/9781009370257
First published online: December 2023

Sara Freeman
University of Puget Sound

Author for correspondence: Sara Freeman, sfreeman@pugetsound.edu

Abstract: Theatre has come back to text, but with perspectives shifted by the experimental practices of the twentieth century across performance forms. Contemporary playwriting brings its scenographic engagement to the foreground of the text, reflecting the spatial turn in theory and practice. In production, this spatiality has renewed and enlivened the status and impact of text-based theatre. Theatre studies need to better describe the artfulness of contemporary text-based theatre, bringing to it the same sophisticated lenses scholars and critics have used for performance-based theatre and other experimental theatre practices. This Element does that by presenting the work of Caryl Churchill, Naomi Iizuka and Sarah Ruhl as exemplary of the way text-based theatre, both its scripts and productions, now creates and expects a spatialized imaginary and demonstrates the potentials of text-based theatre in an increasingly visual and spatial field of cultural production.

This Element also has a video abstract: www.cambridge.org/freeman

Keywords: contemporary playwriting, space and the spatial turn, Caryl Churchill, Naomi Iizuka, Sarah Ruhl

ISBNs: 9781009467940 (HB), 9781009370226 (PB), 9781009370257 (OC)
ISSNs: 2753-2798 (online), 2753-278X (print)

Contents

Introduction – Setting the Scene: Plays and Playwrights

The reinvigorated phenomenology of text-based theatre should rate among the most vital developments in contemporary performance. In the twentieth century, performance theory and the concept of postdramatic theatre seemed to suggest that the key developments in theatre defied and transcended the logocentrism of playwriting. Contemporary playwriting, however, markedly mobilizes text for a spatial imaginary, scenographically, even on the page. This Element analyzes the text and production of one play each by Caryl Churchill, Naomi Iizuka and Sarah Ruhl to explicate the larger currents around playwriting and space. Churchill, Iizuka and Ruhl are all illustrative examples of some of the most distinctive elements of twentieth- and twenty-first-century playwriting in both the United States and the UK. The analysis here focuses on the scenographic aspects of contemporary playwriting, which are its phenomenological and spatial dimensions.

Churchill, Iizuka and Ruhl's work exemplifies the way contemporary playwrights compress the linguistic and imagistic aspects of theatre for phenomenological and spatial impact, and how text-based theatre continues to be a site of great artistic vitality in our vastly expanded performance landscape. I have linked these three writers together because their works so often move into production through an unofficial network of influence connecting them through their collaborators. The direction of Les Waters and design of Annie Smart in particular make a relationship between the three writers in terms of scenography and *mise-en-scene*. This points to a through-line about the phenomenological and spatial dimensions of their writing and how that quality of their work engages collaborating artists. Smart suggested to me that her point of connection for the quality of writing represented by these writers is Gaston Bachelard's (1994) treatise *The Poetics of Space* (first published 1958).[1] Importantly, Scott Cummings's *The Theatre of Les Waters: More Like the Weather* (2022) contains short pieces from all three playwrights alongside many others that track, in an evanescent, self-reflexive way, this shared spatial–phenomenological through-line in the contemporary new writing theatre to which Waters has primarily dedicated his career.

Churchill, Iizuka and Ruhl are associatively and analytically linked in other ways as well. In her analysis of the "two traditions" of contemporary theatre in *Postdramatic Theatre and Form* (2019), Elinor Fuchs cites the plays of both Churchill and Ruhl as examples of the way that elements of the text-based

[1] Smart introduced me to Bachelard's *Poetics of Space* during a guest artist visit to the University of Puget Sound in 2015, noting that it was the book that most helped her find her way as a designer for new writing early in her career.

tradition and the performance-based tradition are co-present in the same works of art. The "story of dramatic and theatrical form is increasingly interesting as the two stands attempt to accommodate each other," she writes (29). Along these lines of combined traditions and shared influences, Sarah Ruhl writes of her experience seeing Churchill's plays in performance and how that transformed her consciousness. For Ruhl, working with Churchill's directorial collaborators Waters and Mark Wing-Davey (who has also staged Iizuka's plays) and heeding Churchill's example was a foundational part of how she continued to learn to be a theatre maker – a collaborator, and a mother, and a political commentator (Ruhl, 2019).

Ruhl's reflections capture her awareness of being part of a lineage, part of a thrust in contemporary theatre practice that simultaneously reinvents forms and vindicates the playwright within the field of practice. The examples she describes of experiencing Churchill's work include watching her mother perform in a production of *Top Girls* (resonating with the genesis of *For Peter Pan*); seeing *Blue Heart* and understanding that language only did part of the work in theatre but also held infinite capacity for experimentation; and of watching the New York premiere of *Far Away* and thinking about both surprise and spectacle in the simultaneity of the production. These insights map exactly onto the scenographic qualities of contemporary writing tracked in the sections of this Element: how plays call for the staging of overlapped worlds and simultaneous realities like in *Top Girls;* the explosion or disintegration of language like in *Blue Kettle*; and the type of self-reflexive consciousness of perception a fully theatrical moment allows, coaxes forth, invites and holds for its audience, like Ruhl experienced watching *Far Away.*

As for Iizuka and Churchill, their plays are frequently anthologized together, as in *Theater of the Avant-Garde 1950–2000: A Critical Anthology* (Knopf and Listengarten, 2011), and they are discussed in parallel in manuals about how to read, stage and design contemporary plays, especially related to the directorial methods of Waters and Wing-Davey.[2] Meanwhile, moving from following the threads of connection following the threads of connection from Churchill to each younger woman to those between Ruhl and Iizuka shows how they travel related career paths in the contemporary US theatre. Though separated by the thin dividing line of a decade's difference in age, they are frequently staged by the same theatres, win the same fellowships or awards within years of each other, or get cited as influences by developing playwrights looking for models.[3]

[2] See *How to Rehearse a Play: A Practical Guide for Directors* (Kiely, 2020), *How to Read a Play: Script Analysis for Directors* (Kiely, 2016) and *Sound and Music for the Theatre: The Art and Technique of Design* (Kaye and LeBrecht, 2015).

[3] See for instance this conversation with emerging playwright Christina Anderson during the 2011 production of *Man in Love* at the 7th Annual First Look Repertory of New Work at Steppenwolf

In 2016, Iizuka and Ruhl were jointly named as the Berlind playwrights-in-residence at the Lewis Center at Princeton University, a move that recognized the McCarter Theatre and Princeton's role in supporting the development of their work early in their careers which between and spoke to their parallel roles within the contemporary playwriting scene.

Together and apart, these three playwrights are justly famous and are already regular subjects of deep literary and performative analysis. Yet, to put playwriting and space together, to read these writers as Smart does, in dialogue with Bachelard, is to read them through a lens that needs more attention in the field of Theatre Studies. Churchill, Iizuka and Ruhl all function as writers in a field where distinctions between text-based and non-text-based work have both opened and closed theatrical pathways for them. Twentieth-century critical theory provided many tools for reading dramatic text and embodied performance, with particular emphasis on ways of dislodging ideological implications and surfacing social and political contexts through analysis. The phenomenological aspects of writing for the theatre, and the spatialized realization of text-based performance, have fewer critical tools. As Julia Jarcho argues in *Writing and the Modern Stage: Theatre beyond Drama* (2020) there is not yet full critical embrace of playwrights as part of the fabric of experimental performance. Sarah Sigal's *Writing in Collaborative Theatre-Making* (2016) explores different strategies for writers who may work with experimental companies (and vice versa), but her sense of process dramaturgy in contemporary theatre making has not fully infused critical treatments of text-based theatre. Concepts of space and spatiality help to reveal how contemporary playwriting works on perception and consciousness and how innovations in playwriting are undoing drama-performance binaries and creating new fusions. Experimental, non-text-based theatre is treated as a spatial act in contemporary analysis. Playwriting is also an act of spatial imagination. Current text-based theatre works as a spatial act as powerfully as non-text-based theatre.

Smart's scenographic embrace of Bachelard's *The Poetics of Space* opens up the role and meaning of text in theatre. This is because Bachelard writes a theory of form, that is, a poetics, that links textuality and spatiality. A poetics is an explanation and vocabulary about what is artful in a medium and how the properties of that medium work on human consciousness if well executed. Bachelard's phenomenology asserts that the human imagination is spatial, that imagination and memory distill our vivid perceptions of embodiment into spatial images. Bachelard addresses questions of freshness, intensity, recognition, wholeness,

Theatre in Chicago: www.steppenwolf.org/articles/man-in-love-playwright-and-director-in-conversation/.

memory and the sacred in relation to the human perception of language and imagery. Bachelard likes to write of "shimmer," the living sense of aesthetic experience and of contact with the soul. For text-based theatre, Bachelard suggests that space is the encounter between the text and the staging.

Working with Bachelard and the parallel sociopolitical aspects of the spatial turn in critical theory outlined in the next section, this Element takes the work of Churchill, Iizuka and Ruhl as outstanding examples of how space matters in contemporary playwriting. Close attention to their work helps reveal how syntheses of text, visuality and physicality manifest more generally in writing from dramatists who collaborate with designers and directors rather than only in the work of artists who bridge or hybridize roles, like director-designers and director-authors such as Joanne Akalitis, Robert Wilson or Richard Foreman. It matters that the careers of these writers and their collaborators span the United States and the UK, because the trends of contemporary playwriting, design and staging are not localized to nations, though this study focuses on anglophone theatre and the changing relationship of text and performance in the postmodern period, which may have different timelines in different national or linguistic traditions and contexts.

In the United States and the UK, the traits of scenographic playwriting are to some degree present in almost three generations of anglophone writers, including waves of writers from the 1970s to the 2010s, notably some of Ruhl's teachers like Maria Irene Fornes and Mac Wellman; playwrights whose work foreshadows Iizuka's like Adrienne Kennedy and Cherie Moraga; and peers of Churchill's like Harold Pinter and of course Howard Barker. Some scenographic aspects of contemporary playwriting reach directly back to the work of Samuel Beckett (McMullen, 2012). Markedly, most twenty-first-century playwrights engage with at least some heightened sense of spatiality – and profit from analysis that attends to it – because there has been a decisive shift in how playwrights target their word artistry for collaboration and staging, participating in postmodern and postdramatic re-ordering and dehierarchization of theatre's expressive elements.

The shows discussed in this Element, all directed and designed by Waters and Smart, shake up theatre's expressive elements even as they present iterations of feminist dramaturgy, documentary theatre and family drama structures. They had first productions that shared a Bachelardian "shimmer" and which mobilized both material and conceptual registers of space in thrilling ways. The plays under consideration are Churchill's *The Skriker* (National Theatre of England, 1994), Iizuka's *At the Vanishing Point* (Actors Theatre of Louisville, 2004 and 2015) and Ruhl's *For Peter Pan on Her 70th Birthday* (Humana Festival of New American Plays and Berkeley Repertory Theatre, 2016). After some more reflection on the context of these works and the nodalities of connection between them in this introduction, the rest of the analysis in this Element employs close textual reading and analysis of my experience in the audience for each play. My direct observation registers the phenomenological impact of the spatiality of the shows, following through on how the scenographic aspects of the writing get realized in production as the writing intertwines with design and direction. As an audience member and scholar, the vivid experiences of these performances propelled me to investigate how text-based theatre shape-shifts because of new modes of theatrical creation and engagement.

While *The Skriker*, *At the Vanishing Point* and *For Peter Pan* span twenty-five years of theatrical trends and developments, they all share ways of foregrounding scenographic aspects and the space-building processes of theatre. First, they each present at least two realities at once. Second, they use fractured language in mimesis-disrupting ways that implicate embodiment and visuality in line with experimental performance traditions. Finally, they require theatrical transformations (*coups de theatre*) that produce intense moments of consciousness in a way that is not just metatheatre, but also the activation of the spatial imagination in Bachelard's mode.

It might seem odd to position *The Skriker* as an exemplar since even in the midst of Churchill's widely varied oeuvre it can feel like an outlier among her shows. Yet, doing so helps capture the way that theatre artists in the 1990s were exploring and bridging the techniques of dramatic writing and live art, movement-based, cross-over and hybrid forms of performance. Churchill's explorations manifest the ways legacies of avant-garde experimentation and collective creation impacted playwriting. Her plays fragment their storytelling and character development in vital and experimental ways, with feminist and eco-critical impact. *The Skriker* comes from a phase of her work where she most actively melded speaking, dancing and singing in collaboration with a director, designer, composer and choreographer. Churchill describes these works as experimental "dance-operas" (Churchill, 1998: viii).

When *The Skriker* premiered in 1994, Churchill could already depend on her reputation for innovation as a dramatist earning her recognition. She stood parallel to Harold Pinter and Tom Stoppard as playwrights who would dazzle in form and content during the late twentieth century. At that point, her use of the backslash and asterisk in dialogue to indicate overlaps and staggered line cuing was most strongly exemplified in *Top Girls* (1982). *Light Shining in Buckinghamshire* (1976) and *Cloud Nine* (1979) featured her brilliant negotiation of history, historicization and Brechtian double-casting displacements. But in her body of work, *The Skriker* rises paramount in a string of plays where she explored a mode of play-building concerned with creating the occasion for perceptual overlaps through the use of text, movement and space configuration which prefigures her sparer works *Far Away* (2000), *A Number* (2002), *Love and Information* (2012) and *Here We Go* (2015).

The Skriker forms a loosely connected trilogy with two other plays of Churchill's that all explore the interaction of the material world and an unseen, spiritual world: *Fen* (1983) and *Mouthful of Birds* (1986). In fact, Churchill's work from 1982 until 1994 included two overlapping "trilogies": there's a triad of works produced at Joint Stock, the Royal Court and the National Theatre – *Fen*, *Mouthful of Birds* and *The Skriker* – for which Ian Spink collaborated as choreographer, Waters directed and Smart was the designer. There's also a triad of works – *Mouthful of Birds*, *The Lives of Great Poisoners* (1991) and *The Skriker* – joined by Churchill's collaboration with the writer and director David Lan and the composers Orlando Gough and Judith Wier. These four plays investigate the embodied dynamics of gender in the experience of economics, sexuality, parenting, justice and mental health. These plays may be her hardest to categorize but are as vital to her profile as her early masterpieces and her later innovations.

As with Churchill's body of work connecting to Joint Stock, the Royal Court and the National Theatre in England, Ruhl and Iizuka's oeuvres are inextricably intertwined with the United States institutions the Berkeley Repertory Theatre and Actors Theatre of Louisville, especially its Humana Festival of New American Plays.[4] These artistic homes are where Churchill, Iizuka and Ruhl's mode of playwriting are brought to fruition in its tradition-blending complexity and not forced into binaries about playwriting, on the one hand, or experimentalism on the other. In *Outrageous Fortune: The Life and Times of the New American Play*, Todd London calls it a default choice to put new plays into small spaces – second stages and studios (London et al., 2009: 187–8). This happens both to protect unknown plays from what in the British context Peter Hall calls "unreasonable" box office pressure and because smaller spaces are often programmed more flexibly than large ones (qtd in Sierz, 2011: 364). The lowered risk also often translates into lowered resources, however, and nonnaturalistic conventions can be hard to do in small spaces with little design support.

In the United States, by the early twenty-first century, new play development programs were very explicitly grappling with the legacy of collective creation, cross-over work and fragmented construction. While experimentation with dramatic form has been a consistent goal of new play production as a category and of movements to encourage new writing for the theatre, ideas about what

[4] Founded in 1977, the Humana Festival of New American Plays at Actors Theatre of Louisville (ATL) continued the post-war goal of raising new playwrights to awareness and supporting new waves of play development and an expansion of styles (Ullom, 2008: 1–10).

a dramatic text might do and what sorts of structures a playwright might employ continued to be contested terrain. New play development programs often found that institutional theatre structures were not well set up to support more open-ended, scenographic dramaturgies. This is the context in which Iizuka's work has most often moved. Many of Iizuka's plays adapt historical, mythological, literary and folkloric material, but *At the Vanishing Point* taps into her seam of quasi-documentary, community-embedded work. Her plays negotiate a complex blend of identity-based, place-based and style-based maneuvers, including an incorporation of documentary theatre techniques and the energies of site-based performance.

In its experimentation, Iizuka's work takes its place among that of nonrealist playwrights like Charles Mee, Len Jenkins, Ruth Margraff, Caridad Svich and Erik Ehn who were opening up form on US stages in the 1990s. She is also part of a generation of global majority playwrights starting to make a mark around the turn of the twenty-first century like Eugenie Chan, Sandra Rogers and Diana Son (Miyagawa, 1997). Esther Kim Lee positions Iizuka as part of a third wave in Asian-American theatre history that rejects all forms of essentialist identity and questions both perception and expectation about identity in their playmaking and performance (2006). Iizuka's early work also appeared in collections about Latino theatre and she is part of the advisory board for the Latino Theatre Commons (Svich and Marrero, 2000).[5]

At the Vanishing Point differs from Iizuka's other works in that it does not appropriate another literary work, though it refers to both myth and Shakespeare. Elsewhere, Iizuka has directly reworked *The Odyssey*, *Agamemnon*, *Hamlet*, *Woyzeck*, Ovid's *Metamorphosis*, plays from Chikamatsu and Japanese folktales, among other sources. *At the Vanishing Point* is also not a play created for or with children, teenagers or college students, which is an aspect of Iizuka's work from *Polaroid Stories* (1997) to *Good Kids* (2014). Instead, the time-looping, haunted interaction with history that *Vanishing Point* pursues resembles *36 Views* (2000) and *Concerning Strange Devices from the Distant West* (2010), but without the direct Asian and Asian-American histories those plays vivify.

At the Vanishing Point may be Iizuka's only play where the historical context and the text itself suggest that the characters are all white. *Polaroid Stories*, *Skin* (1995) and *Tattoo Girl* (1994) function mythically, with not always racially demarcated characters, yet production history shows them to be frequently cast with ensembles made up of actors from a range of racial and ethnic

[5] See also http://howlround.com/showcase-of-the-new-american-theatre-latinao-theatre-commons-carnaval-2015.

backgrounds. In other situations, when Iizuka writes specific political and community histories, the subject matter often intertwines with her own Latina and Asian heritage. *At the Vanishing Point* treats Kentucky with the same ethnographic, community-based engagement found in some of her other place-based work.[6] This gives Louisville's history a similar mythic and metaphysical nonlinearity to that at work in *Polaroid Stories* and *Anonymous* (2006).

Ruhl's plays do not trouble the notion of form quite as aggressively as Churchill's and Iizuka's do, nor are they as thoroughly fractured in structure, but they employ circularities, repetitions and mirrorings that mean that the story of the play may be attenuated even as its phenomenological impact is profound. Ruhl's play structures invite comparisons with musical or poetic forms. She divides *For Peter Pan*, for instance, into three "movements" rather than acts. Across the board Ruhl's plays make people laugh, but they insist on talking about mortality and heartbreak, and her experimentalism can be underestimated (Al-Shamma, 2011).[7] In the second half of her career, Ruhl has shifted from writing what might be called father and lover plays to writing marriage and mother plays. Written as a gift for Ruhl's mother, but still deeply concerned with the presence and absence of fathers, *For Peter Pan* may represent the best synthesis of these two strands in her work. Ruhl and her reception represent the complete mainstream embrace of a postmodern and postdramatic stylistic eclecticism made possible by five decades of sustained artistic, dramaturgical and educational commitment to expanding the role and aesthetic range of new plays in anglophone theatre.

Ruhl's signature is the blending of the real and surreal, which is accomplished with a type of brilliant lightness around space, language and image. Her peers include Lisa Loomer, Jenny Schwartz, Kate Fodor, Young Jean Lee, Julia Jordan, Quiara Alegria Hudes and Kia Cothron, but she also takes her place in comparison to writers who were her teachers, specifically Paula Vogel, Maria Irene Fornes, Nilo Cruz and Mac Wellman (Durham, 2013; Ruhl, 2001). *For Peter Pan on Her 70th Birthday* begins with a deceptively prosaic first section for a piece by a playwright associated with a theatrical version of magic realism. Ruhl's play creates an uncanny seeming-like realism: it feels recognizable and then it slips away into something else. The play feigns to be almost purely

[6] Such as *100 Years After* (2008) and *Ghostwritten* (2009) which treat the history of Cambodian genocide and the Vietnam war; *17 Reasons Why* (2003), driven by histories of the residents of San Francisco's Mission District; and *3 Truths* (2010) which took on California border and immigration histories as part of Cornerstone Theatre's Justice Cycle.

[7] Al-Shamma discusses Ruhl's postmodern asynchronicity and intertextuality, though it strikes me that he misses how her plays resonate in space once designed and staged, so he characterizes her as fairly "traditional" in her treatment of plot, character and agon because he does not consider the plays as fully in space (186).

naturalistic, almost happening in real time. Several of Ruhl's other plays also begin as if they were more conventional plays, a contemporary comedy with *The Clean House* (2004), an Ibsenesque drama with *In the Next Room* (2009), a backstage drama with *Stage Kiss* (2014). Others, like *Melancholy Play* (2002) or *Late: A Cowboy Song* (2003) announce their stylistic departures immediately.

From 2001 to 2017, Ruhl was in a near-constant state of production around the United States at every type of theatre committed to developing new plays, at the rate of what seemed like a new play each year or more. Each work concocted transformational outcomes from familial and romantic encounters. Her plays differ from some naturalistic waves of new play development in US theatre because they recast the balance between seriousness and whimsy with spatiality, metatheatricality and an embrace of embedded performance experiments. *For Peter Pan*, in specific, employs an assemblage of devices that include direct address, ritual behavior, the presence of a live dog and marching band and special effects sequences for flying.

It's tempting to read *For Peter Pan* as the inversion of *Eurydice* (2003), the play that first cemented Ruhl's theatrical fame. *Eurydice* features a young main character while *For Peter Pan* does quite the opposite. In one, death means a journey to the underworld; in the other, death means a transcendent flight. *Eurydice*'s Nasty Interesting Man is Freudian, grotesque and compelling; *Peter Pan*'s Captain Hook is burlesque and almost pathetic. Eurydice's ghost father arrives in a noble revelation when Eurydice makes peace with her own death; the ghost father in *For Peter Pan* is the surprise of the second act, creating comic impact, his presence never perceived by Ann. Eurydice and her father build a framing of string to house their mourning, while Ann and her siblings mourn in a too-too solid house.

Yet the connections between the two shows suggest that together they form the synthesis of her treatment of death, memory and transcendent family love. The earlier play employs a chorus of stones, a much more abstract move than the reanimation of *Peter Pan* with sexagenarians, yet both choices theatricalize processes of grief and self-transformation. While the psychosexual tension of *Eurydice* gives way to a late-life existential crisis in *For Peter Pan*, both plays turn on the loss of a father and moments of deep self-knowledge. *Eurydice* makes peace in death with forgetting; *For Peter Pan* probes the leap of faith that crossing over will require even while remembering. Ovidean metamorphosis and the sentimentalism of J. M. Barrie suit different life-stages, and Ruhl's genius structures plays where death is never the end.

Out of all of Ruhl's work, these two texts, along with *Orlando* (1998), are the ones most about time and death. *The Skriker* and *At the Vanishing Point* are about death too, though perhaps the most correct thing to say is that their scenographic aspects are about transformation across times and states of being, of which death is one. The language and intensifications of consciousness in these plays demonstrate the ways contemporary playwrights meld the text-based and the performance-based tradition of the twentieth century and heighten the possibilities of dramatic form.

Having set this scene, the following sections of the Element continue to define the scenographic aspects of contemporary playwriting and assert that contemporary text-based theatre is also written into space. Section 1 connects different parts of the spatial turn in critical theory and establishes that spatiality is a better concept than visuality to explain the dynamics of new plays. Section 1 begins to unfold how the integrated conceptual and concrete way spatial perception works gets activated by the dialogue, design and direction of contemporary playwriting. Sections 2, 3 and 4 analyze specific plays and productions by Churchill, Iizuka and Ruhl in that integrated conceptual and concrete way, showing how they reorder or dehierarchize theatre's the expressive elements and activate the spatial imagination as part of shaking up audience perception and dramatic form.

1 Playwriting and Space

Theatre has come back to text in the twenty-first century but with perspectives shifted by experimental practices across performance forms. The phenomenological and spatiotemporal dimensions of playwriting have taken on increased importance as text-based and performance-based traditions intertwine (Fuchs, 2019). Playwrights are fully embedded in an artistic and cultural milieu that has assimilated the insights of a century of formal experimentation in literature, the visual arts, media and theatre; the techniques of auteur directors; and the processes of ensemble creation (Sigal, 2016). Now, playwrights have as much, or more, in common with performance artists and scenographers as with any other type of artist. The dramaturgical attributes of contemporary plays are in dialogue with and informed by the same potentials for spatiality and embodiment that performance experiments, past and present, use to resist dramatic text, resist logocentrism and resist even received ideas about theatre as an art form (Jarcho, 2020; Radosavljevic, 2013; Tomlin, 2013).

For an earlier generation of critics, contrasting a "theatre of images" to the traditional theatre of text was a way to describe innovations in form pursued by hyphenate director-designer-writers like Robert Wilson, Richard Foreman and Lee Breuer after the 1960s (Marranca, 1977). This contrast highlighted overreliance on text and restrictive notions of authorship that could deaden or constrain the use of theatre's full range of expressive elements in comparison to other artistic mediums and modes of experimental performance. Contemporary scripts now read differently than scripts created when the text/image contrast was new. Contemporary plays live on the stage differently as well. Contemporary writing reflects a spatial sensibility in theatre, mobilizing, recovering and reinventing text as part of visuality and physicality, of spatiotemporal play and transformational theatre magic, rather than having the text establish the limit or opposite of those aspects of performance.

Space and spatiality constitute important elements for understanding the combination of text, visuality, composition and embodiment in contemporary playwriting. Space is both a felt relationship in the material world and a conceptual way of engaging the perceiving consciousness. Space is both concrete and conceptual as an element of theatre; spatiality is the encounter between text and staging. The marriage of the concrete and the conceptual is a scenographic way of understanding space as part of theater artistry. Scenography is the "space building processes" of theatre (Kipp, 2018: 250). Contemporary playwriting brings scenographic engagement to the foreground, reflecting the spatial turn in cultural theory and artistic practice. Contemporary playwrights engage with the same set of concerns about the "manipulation and orchestration of the performance environment" wherein "space is the main object of creation" and space is "the agent in the creation of multiple realities" that drives scenography (McKinney and Butterworth, 2009: 4, 124). The spatiality of contemporary plays has renewed and enlivened the processes, status and impact of text-based theatre after a period where writers were sometimes positioned as expendable and "text-based" theatre could be seen as a retrograde or limiting form of performance, lacking the transformational aspects of postdramatic theatre and experimental performance.

One point of evidence about the relationship of space and contemporary anglophone writing is that processes around the development of new plays now attend to the scenographic totality the written text will enter and that playwrights aim to collaborate in creating. In a panel about design and dramaturgy at the 2015 Literary Managers and Dramaturgs of the Americas (LMDA) conference, designer Rachel Hauk described the "dream design" process at the Eugene O'Neill Theatre Center during its annual summer theatre lab for new plays. Hauck ! noted that the designer's negotiation of text and image with the playwright is one of the first things that happens in that process. The designers take the script that the playwright knows "so intimately" and change the writer's perspective on it; she said, "coming at it from the back and the side, which is what designers do."[8] Hauck said those conversations form a shared vocabulary around the imagery and spatiality of the play. Spatialized modes of "conceiving the forms" of a play like this have increased the expansiveness with which text can be received, recognized and mobilized across the work of directors, designers and playwrights (Devin, 1997). Playwrights definitively do not just write a script that hermetically contains all the imaginative resources needed anymore, if they ever did. This means script readers and evaluators also must come to embrace the spaces suggested in contemporary writing.

Confirming this shift, during the 2016 Fertile Ground festival in Portland, Oregon, Mead Hunter, who was artistic director of the New Harmony Project from 2011 until 2018, presented as part of a panel session on new works development. He observed a sea-change at New Harmony across three decades of work with theatre writers, sharing that "we've come to realize now that most of the exciting work looks very, very underwritten on the page, leaving lots of room for other collaborators."[9] New Harmony has been "very, very literary for most of its history," Hunter noted, suggesting that the labs worked with an attitude that implied: "Submit a script and it's a literary artifact." But that's not how plays are getting created or staged now, Hunter affirmed. The relationship between text and staging, always dynamic, continues to evolve, but a spatialized imaginary, or even a Bachelardian poetics of space, is pulling up equal to a literary poetics.

Analysis exists of the "scenographic playwriting" or "scenographic dramaturgy" of artists who direct and design the plays they've written, like Foreman and Howard Barker, or who construct works as director-designers using fragments of text, actor-generated sequences or some of their own writing like Wilson, Joanne Akalitis and Robert LePage (Aronson, 2005; Kipp, 2018; Poll, 2018). Works in this mode are sometimes described as being "written into space" (Saivetz, 2000). Current text-based theatre is also written into space by its collaborative team with playwrights doing their part to inspire and support how theatre's expressive elements work together in space. Many leading playwrights of the last thirty years create work that is narrative but fractured; that is non-realist and relies on nonverbal signification and non-dialogic language to disrupt mimesis while still reflecting

[8] "Design and Dramaturgy" panel at the LMDA Annual Conference, June 27, 2015, Columbia University, New York. New York. Panelists: Fitz Patton, Martha Skeketee, Rachel Hauck and Louisa Thompson. Moderator Vicki Stroich. All further quotations from this panel come from the author's notes from attending and the HowlRound TV video stream, available on the LMDA webpage https://lmda.org/design-and-dramaturgy.

[9] Sara Freeman, notes from January 26, 2016 panel "Development of New Work in Institutions," at the Fertile Ground Festival, Portland, Oregon, observed by Skype, with notes from Jessica Wallenfells, moderator. Panelists: Ben Feinstein, Lue Douthit, Mead Hunter, LuAnn Spooler.

human behavior in ways that are representational. Contemporary playwriting tends to anticipate and require a visuality and physicality in design and *mise-en-scene* that makes non-textual elements equal in the storytelling, sensation-production and event-making of their plays.

This Element analyzes one play each from Caryl Churchill, Naomi Iizuka and Sarah Ruhl to exemplify these overall trends; they are examples of playwrights also writing theatre's expressive elements into space. The plays under consideration – both their texts and first productions – draw on and meld the innovations of physical theatre, verbatim plays, auteur direction and postmodern ensemble creation in their play-making and script composition. These three shows in particular, *The Skriker* (1994), *At the Vanishing Point* (2004 and 2015) and *For Peter Pan on Her 70th Birthday* (2016), open, complicate and distill theatrical storytelling in multidirectional, spatialized ways. Their writing synthesizes performance experiments recognizable from the work of solo performance artists, physical theatre companies, body-based performance, performance lectures, installation and site-based performance, and continues to challenge traditional play construction or the over-prioritization of theatre texts as literature.

In particular, the treatment of time and space in Churchill, Iizuka and Ruhl's work demonstrates the scenographic aspects of contemporary play-writing. The spatiotemporal shifting of contemporary texts manifests in the nature of language, the use of stage directions and the perceptual play of consciousness they create; their appeal to a spatial imaginary occurs both on the page and on the stage, as something to experience. This encounter extends beyond metatheatrical self-reflexivity because the goal is not mainly to disclose the artistic status of the dramatic or theatrical construct to the audience through ritual or role-playing or referentiality, but rather to activate human senses, memory and understanding in the way spatial perception does. Since contemporary playwriting is permeated, as Liz Tomlin puts it, "by the deconstruction of language and the turn to the experiential"(2013: viii), space-sensitive performance analysis is necessary for understanding contemporary performance texts. The spatial turn in critical theory aids in this way of reading text-based work.

The Spatial Turn

Henri LeFevre describes space as a medium of cultural expression. The spatial turn in critical theory focuses on the analysis of this medium of cultural expression. The spatial turn branches in two related directions. One direction focuses on the phenomenology of spatial imaginaries activated by expressive elements in art and literature, as exemplified by Gaston Bachelard's *The Poetics of Space* (1994); the other, as in the works of Lefebvre (1991), Michel Foucault (1986), Yi-Fu Tuan (1977), Doreen Massey (1994) and Michel DeCerteau (1984), probes the social construction of space, opening up where power relations are embedded and performed in the material experiences and conceptual structures of a society. The spatial turn in cultural and aesthetic theory helps explain how audiences "read" space as they experience a play, attending to all the expressive scenographic and poetic elements of theatre while engaging with the cultural and political meanings evoked by configurations of those elements.

The scenographic aspects of contemporary playwriting resonate with both Bachelardian-phenomenological and socio-critical approaches to space because of the nature of theatre's expressive elements and how they impact audiences. The expressive elements of theatre are multisensory and encourage phenomenological engagement: they include architectural structures, light, projections, sound, costumes, performance objects and props and compositional, body-based arrangements of gesture, proxemics, silhouette and pose, as well as poetic, storytelling structures like plot, character, theme and language. The use of color, texture, shape, mass, weight, line, focus, balance, pattern, brightness, shadow, height, depth and scale in the expressive elements call on spatial perception. Meanwhile, the spatialized registers of social power structures that audiences apprehend in the performance's form and content result in audience experiences that are spatial both analytically and imaginatively. Space as a critical concept illuminates both the choices artists make and the meanings audiences take, both production and reception, for a work of theatre.

Here it is worth clarifying that spatiality and visuality are not precisely the same thing. Space is multisensory, while visuality could be reduced to those things perceived by looking alone. Space is the better term for what is at stake in theatre because of the integrated conceptual and concrete way spatial perception works. However, the visual aspects of theatre are often what are being lifted up when critics note that text or language as an element of dramatic theatre is overemphasized in comparison to other expressive elements. Thus, the phrase "visual dramaturgy" keeps gaining currency to talk about the properties of contemporary performance because the contrast between word and image highlights critical concerns about textuality and visuality.

In Hans-Thies Lehmann's work and critical writing by Knute Ove Arntzen, the phrase visual dramaturgy arises as a way of describing how a performance might be structured if it is not "controlled" or "ordered" by text, or an Aristotelian poetics of plot and character (Arntzen, 1991; Lehmann, 2006). Theatre artists also often use "visual dramaturgy" to invoke shared creative vocabularies among a production team. Lucas Krech's article "Towards an Understanding of Visual Dramaturgy," for instance, "positions the theatre designer as a translator between the non-visual text and the visual theatre performance" (2010). Arntzen deployed the first published use of the phrase by evoking a "visual type of dramaturgy" to discuss approaches to theatre where "elements or means of expression, such as space, frontality, textuality and visuality, are no longer arranged in the traditional sense of organic or hierarchic systems, but are equivalent, on an equal footing" (1991). Lehmann named visual dramaturgy as a component of postdramatic theatre, noting that the visual aspect of postdramatic performance is not "subordinated to the text," but "free to develop its own logic" (2006: 93). Lehmann and others initially didn't think that the author-function of playwrights in text-based work allowed much room for visual dramaturgy, but contemporary playwriting has absorbed postdramatic experimentation as well, mobilizing text in and as part of the overall visuality and spatiality of contemporary forms.

As the notion of visual dramaturgy infiltrates new play development organizations and playwriting techniques, it names a more nonhierarchical approach to the relationship between theatre's expressive elements in a particular work, across a body of work or in collaborative processes. In their article, "Visual Dramaturgy: Problem Solver or Problem Maker in Contemporary Performance Creation," Cat Gleason, Wes Pearce, Martine Kei Green-Rogers and Justin Maxwell analyze what the phrase visual dramaturgy suggests about the nature of contemporary play texts and performance creation (Pearce et al., 2018). In particular, Pearce as a designer suggests that visual dramaturgy is to scenography as dramaturgy is to playwriting, leaving open the relationship of playwriting to scenography. Maxwell as a playwright writes of being a "language artist in a visual medium," of being "an artist who works in language in the same way a painter works in pigments or a musician in sounds," which resonates with how many contemporary playwrights approach their craft. Mara Irene Fornes, for instance, was known to describe playwriting as a mode of "painting with words" (López, 2016: 100).[10] Perhaps it is best to say that the visual dramaturgy of contemporary writing re-spatializes text as part of theatre. The tactic employed in this analysis is to respond to the phenomenological aspects of both the playwriting and the scenography in the first production of *The Skriker*, *At the Vanishing Point* and *For Peter Pan*, addressing both their dramaturgy and their visual dramaturgy as modes of space-creation. Playwriting is also a spatial act and text-based theatre revitalizes itself anew every time the relationship of text and space is deepened or expanded.

[10] For more on the connection between playwriting and design in contemporary theatre, see also the *American Theatre* article about Fornes's "acute sense of design" and her collaboration with designers (Regan, 2017).

The sociopolitical branch of the spatial turn in critical theory prizes the way a performance can shift perception to envision re-orderings of power structures. This angle of analysis emphasizes the cultural and political insight that emerges from the way a piece of theatre can shift perception. Joanne Tompkins's book *Theatre's Heterotopias: Performance and the Cultural Politics of Space*, for instance, tracks the way that theatre productions "rehearse spaces of possibility" between the Lefevrian constructed space of society and the abstracted space of aesthetic experience (2014: 37). Tompkins establishes how audiences can experience and reflect on the critique of existing social orders in a performance, or imagine into being a changed social order. Alternative re-orderings of social structures and alternative re-orderings of expressive elements join in contemporary playwriting, foregrounding and heightening the scenographic aspects of contemporary playwriting.

The scenographic aspects of contemporary playwriting may have become more legible across the last thirty years because the spatial turn has opened up discussions of visual dramaturgies that contravene hierarchical orderings of theatre's expressive elements that used to, by default, place writer, word, language and text at the top of an authorial hierarchy. Churchill, Iizuka and Ruhl are commonly read by critics as playwrights whose plots, characters and themes convey powerful re-orderings of social and political structures; like much of contemporary playwriting, their work encourages the reimagination of social orders. This study mainly focuses, therefore, on the multisensory phenomenological register of their theatre-making, text and staging. Their examples demonstrate how playwrights now enscript a playful and potent range of alternative re-orderings of theatre's expressive elements. In the rest of this section, there is a consideration of the ways the texts of the plays are themselves shifting spatiotemporal constructions. The subsequent overview on language, embodiment and the perception of consciousness in the shows lay out the groundwork for the case studies in Sections 2–4.

Space and Time

One of the most arresting scenographic aspects of Churchill, Iizuka and Ruhl's writing is its presentation of at least two overlapped and simultaneous realities at once. This characteristic, along with their approaches to language, shakes up linearities of form and narrative. The two worlds, two times or two planes of existence can be described in terms of both space and time. In *The Skriker* there is the (human) world and the (fairy) underworld: these descriptions imply they are spatially above and below each other, but in production, staging renders them as overlapped, happening in the same space. Yet, characters can also be whisked from one to the other. As temporal phenomena, the human world and the underworld are co-present, but time can pass faster or much slower in the fairy world as compared to the human world – being whisked from one to the other may result in temporal displacement far into the future or the experience of long-endured time passing when no time has passed for others.

In *At the Vanishing Point*, the two realities are that of the past and the present: of the Butchertown neighborhood in Louisville, Kentucky at multiple points in time, particularly the 1930s, the 1970s and a "now" of 2015. In those times, the play presents details of artist Ralph Eugene Meatyard's biography and family story and the memories of residents of Butchertown, as well as recovered history of the neighborhood and imaginative recreation of events. Timewise, the play's doubleness comes from the overlapping of memories spatially, it is also now and the past, here and not here: Butchertown as it exists today is just down the block from the theatre, while on stage its past is made present again with images, bodies and words. *For Peter Pan's* three realities concern life, the afterlife and the theatre: Ruhl magnifies the metaphysical aspects of her play with a triple layering. Spatially, the living and the dead of *For Peter Pan* share the rooms of a hospital and a family house; temporally the play presents both a lived now, a narrated looking back and an imagined flight set in the theatre.

Layering, superimposition and simultaneity in the presentation of space and time seem like aesthetic qualities driven by joining or a mixing of elements, but on the contrary, in text and in performance they operate as a mode of separation that challenges naturalistic conventions and forces apart the sense of unified storytelling. The simultaneous realities of Churchill, Iizuka and Ruhl mean the design and direction do not present a seamless onstage "now" in which action happens; likewise they mean that the revelation of information may not be sequential, or, even if it is, later revelations will alter both the characters and the audiences' attitude toward that knowledge. If the time/space on stage bends, or just has more dimensions visible at once than are available in offstage life, it shifts the frontier between representation and reality in a way that Patrice Pavis suggests works like installation art (2013: 57).

In this, these shows participate in the "metaphysical turn" Chris Megson describes in contemporary playwriting, which has "moved beyond systems of naturalist stage representation by calibrating a different experience of time" (2013: 34). Churchill shatters naturalist temporal logic by jumping through time in *The Skriker*, while in *For Peter Pan*, Ruhl begins with naturalistic stage conventions for time, and then dissolves them into a no-time dream-time. Iizuka, perhaps because of *At the Vanishing Point*'s explicit presentation of history, most employs the sense of all time held in an instant, positing the stage as a place that can hold objective, factual information and the emotional, individual sense of those events simultaneously.

Calibrating different experiences of time evokes adjustment, mixing and arranging elements together, composing them into a compound or configuration. Churchill, Iizuka and Ruhl do this with their representation of space and time, and, in turn, when their plays are staged, this representation of space-time takes on specific aspects related to scale. These three plays are notably big. This bigness speaks to their reworking of naturalism; it also challenges expectations about new writing for the theatre and how it will be designed and directed. Often, plays toying with space and time are in need of both scale and some theatrical magic. Contemporary playwriting at its most innovative asks for and mobilizes that scale and spatiality.

Language and Embodiment

Churchill, Iizuka and Ruhl's use of language is so elegant that it can hide how experimental they are being. Their language is precise, surprising, taut and sensuous, but it also slips from conveying the plot and characters into being a voice itself, joining the visuality and physicality of the play to both propel and disrupt mimesis. Language in these plays does not primarily represent the world (*mimesis*), though it does that too. These playwrights employ dialogue that allows characters to pursue their action and the story to unfold, and all three of them have an ear for the flows and interruptions of daily speech. But the primary function of language in their shows is to be dazzling and rhythmic as part of interacting with or propelling types of visuality and physicality. These writers break open the functions of language on the page by refusing or repurposing punctuation and capitalization, upsetting sequence and syntax and forming complex repetitions or elisions. This impacts how the layout of their texts looks; it is a mode of textual decomposition. It also impacts physical embodiment and the approach to the composition of stage pictures.

Assessing contemporary playwriting, Aleks Sierz reflects "[p]erhaps the best plays are those that mix naturalistic dialogue with a more left field theatrical imagination," suggesting that it is the decomposition of realist conventions that propels the most satisfying formal experimentation in text-based theatres (2008: 107). Naturalistic dialogue sounds like everyday speech, and since in everyday life people are often at a loss for words or unable to speak eloquently, that speech isn't always rhetorically or poetically beautiful. Churchill, Iizuka and Ruhl trouble that second sense of naturalistic dialogue because the language they employ often exceeds the needs of the characters and moves the storytelling into registers where the language also participates in the "left field theatrical imagination."

Another place to see this is the stage directions. Malgoreta Sugiera writes that the distinction between dialogue and stage directions is receding in contemporary Polish, British and German plays where

> even if they observe the widely-accepted distinction between the primary text and the stage directions, and stick to the traditional pattern of scripting dialogical cues, each of them introduced with the name of the speaker, it does not follow immediately that they still imitate on stage interpersonal relationships in compliance with the expectations and the perceptual habits of the majority of the spectators (2004: 18).

Ruhl, in general, does stick to the traditional pattern of scripting dialogical cues, while with Churchill and Iizuka it varies by play. Some have few dialogical cues or no specified speakers, while others may have specified speakers, but work through the juxtaposition of long passages rather than dialogue. For all three writers, the modes of staging interpersonal relationships include a reliance on spoken subtext, symbolic behavior, dance and retroactive narration that exceed the sense of simply watching human beings act in real time primarily by speaking to one another. Their stage directions especially highlight the role of language in their theatrical experimentalism.

In *The Skriker*, the paucity of stage directions proves most notable and puts the emphasis on one set of stage directions related to an aspect of the overlapped human and fairy worlds the play presents. Churchill does not break up the play by acts and scenes. The text presents one long flow of dialogue with designations about when characters enter or exit and simple descriptions of physical sequences and the look of characters. Because the Skriker is a shape-shifter, the stage directions recurrently describe a "new" figure onstage and then declare "It is the Skriker." Otherwise, Churchill reserves her stage directions for indicating pauses and spare descriptions of movement that nod toward the type of choreography created by Ian Spink for the show in the first production or phrases conjuring the bad glamour of the underworld. However, one run of notes is particularly marked. It begins with "a Passerby comes along the street, throws down a coin, and then starts to dance to the music" and then continues with nine instances of a version of the phrase "the Passerby is still dancing" (252–91). The variation ranges from "the Passerby never stops dancing" to the final text in the play which is: "the Passerby stops dancing." In other words, ten pages in the text indicates that a body begins dancing, and then periodically reminds readers that it doesn't stop until the end of the play. On stage, this dancing body is continuously present (or made to seem so by the staging) and signaling in a way that stage directions can in no way capture. This isn't an "impossible" stage direction, but it does set up a theatrical demand that shakes up any sense of surety about what the text can communicate without the dancing.[11] This project of fully integrating the physical and the verbal is at the heart of Churchill's writerly concerns in *The Skriker* as she probes the limits of language for conveying bodily presence.

By contrast, even given the sense of restraint in her writing, Iizuka's stage directions in *At the Vanishing Point* form a type of persistent narration. The text comes in large monologic chunks, and after almost every paragraph there is a long stage direction. Two-thirds of the way through the play, as the play winds up for its crescendo, there is a very long stage direction that discusses flashes of light and types of music and sound effects as well as movement of the actors. This also contains a litany of facts about Butchertown to be whispered during this sequence of sound effects and movement. The passage culminates with "as the facts are read, the BOY in the clothes from the last century emerges from the darkness. the GIRL in the white dress follows him. they play orpheus and eurydice. the BOY walks ahead of the GIRL" (Iizuka, 2015: 24). Iizuka's decomposition of capitalization accompanies her larger experiments with language as a part of immersive sensory experience, where the solidity of the characters is deemphasized and the audience's consciousness is encouraged into the character's perception so the vividness of the imagery becomes more visceral. The storm sequence in *Vanishing Point* features a potent stage direction where language works like a spell, an incantation that delivers historical information and also conjures immersive stage effects.

Ruhl's stage directions move from narration to take on an interrogative, exploratory tone. This is one aspect of her dramaturgy much remarked on: the extraordinary, improbable things proposed in her stage directions, but *proposed* rather than described or required. Ruhl's stage directions are like having a collaborative conversation – whether with her, or with the spirit of the play. The stage directions often say "if" or "perhaps" or, even, "or." Even before the script begins, in her author's notes, the voice of Ruhl's stage directions establishes itself. *For Peter Pan* begins with a sentence that matters a great deal to stage design and staging the space: "*If there is no actual flying, one can imagine beautiful painted backdrops that make you think the actors are flying.*" Later, at the end of Act I, the stage direction proposes:

> *If they play instruments, they might now form a rag-tag 5 piece band with trumpet and accordion and sing and play "When the Saints Go Marching In."*
> *Or a marching band might enter.*
> *Or they might just sing the song, with some home-spun attempts at harmony.*
> *And push the hospital bed off, ceremonially.* (Ruhl, 2018: 34)

[11] Consider Mark Lawson's praise of impossible stage directions in *The Guardian* www.theguardian.com/stage/2012/jun/12/stage-directions-dead-end; see also Karen Quigley (2020), which is in part about stage directions.

The stage directions go from describing a group of siblings saying the Lord's Prayer together such that "the prayer becomes a song" to proposing how they get to singing since the next dialogue is the lyrics of "When the Saints Go Marching In." Ruhl's exploratory stage directions are part of an experimental rendering into dramatic text an open-ended sense of what might work for staging and an invitation to the spatial imagination.

Decomposing language creates gaps and the playwrights use it to create flexibility, mobility or immersion. Maxwell's sense of himself as a "language artist in a visual medium" resounds here and frames Churchill, Iizuka and Ruhl's writing as part of contemporary explorations of theatre's properties as a medium. How far can dramatic storytelling go in space? How does language mobilize our spatial imaginations? What does it do to our perception?

Perception of Consciousness

Contemporary playwriting complicates naturalism and realism to create a particular trajectory of transformed consciousness. Most current writing extends beyond a realist invitation to observe and reflect on the patterns and materiality of the world or epic theatre's invitation to consider social context and political constructs functioning in the world. Instead, the self-reflective, scenographic quality of contemporary plays foregrounds an awareness of consciousness in the moment, of the world-creating power of a perceiving, embodied mind – a type of quantum sensibility around consciousness. Many dramaturgical structures for plays center the revelation of information; in contemporary playwriting, the central concern is to create the space to witness a transformation.[12]

Witnessing a transformation creates compelling opportunities for *coups de theatre*, a term used to describe those triumphs of staging and design that thrill, delight, terrify or haunt the audience and which often synthesize the most shattering turns or revelations the performance has to offer. Each of the plays under consideration features a *coup de theatre* that makes the most of theatrical transformations, the type of theatricality that invites renewed or shifted consciousness. In *The Skriker*, for example, in the final moment of the play, the character Lily returns to the human world from the underworld to discover not, as she expected, that no time had passed, but rather, that hundreds of years had passed. At that moment, she encounters her daughter's granddaughter. The

[12] Classical and realist plays can be staged to highlight transformations and this type of self-reflective consciousness (and sometimes allow a director to do so with more impunity as to how the words factor in) which is why revivals of classics continue to be a major factor in contemporary theatre, just as plays from antiquity and previous centuries could be and were consistently restaged to emphasize realist and epic emphases throughout the twentieth century.

quantum leap into a desolate future, staged as if it were on the surface of the moon, disorients character and spectator alike, creating a sense of expansion, fear, dislocation and eternity, all in a moment. The transformations and disintegrations of the scripted language and the *coups de theatre* set up by the playwrights make these contemporary plays both memory houses and social maps, Bachelardian spatializations of imagination and insight.

The ends of each of these plays bend perception and open spaces of possibility. *At the Vanishing Point* ends simply, with the stage directions asking for the effect of "sunlight on water" and Maudie Totten echoing the Photographer's earlier invocation of the totality of living a "whole, entire life." She says she is thinking of "all the things i have no words for, all the things alive in that precise point in time, the tiniest things" (31–2). She speaks to the tiniest things, but the effect of that moment, her glory even in the absence of words, is to encompass all the stories told that evening, to allow them to shimmer in the light, as if everything were there, in that moment all at once. *For Peter Pan* ends with the character Ann, who is also our Peter Pan, reliving her teenage performance of a traditional version of Barrie's *Peter Pan* and her conversation with her father backstage. This actually happened in the months before she left for college, but the conversation is also an anticipation of her own death. Ann in this moment is both Ann and Pan, both mythic and daily, echoing *The Skriker*'s combination of the human and beyond-human reality. As the third movement of the play ends, she hugs her father across all time and space and watches him go. An epilogue follows, and Ann says that in the past, when she was young, she took off her Peter Pan tights (though she does not take them off onstage) but that she stayed in the theatre, meaning she left behind her role, but she stayed in the perceptual space opened by theatre. The stage directions say: "*She throws a handful of pixie dust. It catches the light. She flies off. A fantastical exit. The end*" (101). The tension between her past and present, her consciousness on the edge of ending, can only be resolved with theatrical magic.

Attentive to that type of magic, the following three sections identify specific spatial and phenomenological dimensions at play in the performance texts by Churchill, Iizuka and Ruhl. *The Skriker*, the story of which springs from myth and folklore, works with the spatial and phenomenological dimensions of superimposition and the positionality of above and below. *At the Vanishing Point* engages site-based specificity through simultaneity and the spatial permeability of that which is in front and that which is behind in the stage picture. *For Peter Pan* emerges from family history, layering it with the spatial and phenomenological dimensions of horizontality and verticality.

2 Caryl Churchill: Shape-shifting and Superimposition

As a text and in its first production, *The Skriker* powerfully depicted transformations in nature, gender and perception in superimposed space of the human world and the fairy underworld. *The Skriker* came at a pivot point between two phases of Churchill's work when what was understood about Churchill's writing, based on her more Brechtian work from the 1970s was being shattered, and her experimentation with dramatic form began a scenographic acceleration. *The Skriker* also came at a shifting point in British theatre's embrace of more experimental dramaturgical structures. Dan Rebellato notes that there were "several perceptual shifts beginning in the mid 1990s characterized by writers abdicating from aspects of their plays that they formerly might have been expected to control," manifesting in dramaturgical choices like: sections of a play that can be performed in any order, no character names, no assignment of time, not assigning lines to characters/actors (2013: 15).

With this, British theatre of the 1990s and beyond saw a spread of playtexts that had a new kind of openness. Rebellato writes about Martin Crimp's *Attempts on Her Life* (1997), Sarah Kane's *Blasted* (1995), Mark Ravenhill's *Shopping and Fucking* (1996) and Simon Stephens's *Pornography* (2007). It is significant that just before the premiere of those 1990s shows, Churchill's experimental dance-text opened at the National Theater in London, anticipating, harnessing and going beyond many of the trends and techniques of contemporary playwriting to come with the younger generation highlighed by Rebellato. My experience watching the show while studying abroad in London forever altered my understanding of what a play could be.

The Skriker is a dance-theatre piece about two working-class teenage mothers in London; they are pursued by an ancient shape-shifting fairy who must feed off the life force of human beings and who is suffering because degradation to the natural world is causing a system breakdown in the environment that sustains them all. It took me three viewings of the show to come to terms with how the play worked. I was thrilled and intrigued. This intrigue captured many spectators who were theatre artists, it seems, as Chloe Veltman writes in *American Theatre* about the cult status of *The Skriker* among a set of theatre makers (2007: 44). *The Skriker* follows the quest of the titular ancient shape-shifter to glamour two disenfranchised teenage mothers, Lily and Josie (Josie has murdered her baby in a fit of postpartum psychosis), feed off their energy and transport them to a dark underworld of mythological and folkloric creatures displaced by modern rationalism and postmodern environmental collapse. However, because the character of the Skriker is a shape-shifter and a speaker of Joycean monologues made of broken and recombined fairytale references and punning turns of phrase, the human-scale presence of Lily and Josie as the center of the plot gets twisted.

The play features a complete overlap of human and fairy world and incorporates near-constant dance, so its need for physical invention and frequent violence overflowed the separation of space created by the large-scale nested boxes that defined Annie Smart's set, which, like her punk rock fairy costumes, transformed rapidly and elegantly.[13] Director Les Waters's production valued the interplay of formal experimentation and psychological insight emerging from how Churchill makes elements of time, place, plot and character plural and shifting, building on the experiments of both feminist theatre and cross-over visual and physical theatre. But, given a high profile by premiering at the National, the show bedeviled critical reception when it opened, because many critics felt they could not discern a plot or argued that the dance and the text did not work together well, positioning the show as sub-Pina Bausch (Brantley, 1996; Caplan, 1994; Remshardt, 1995).

For me, though, the effect was primal, shaking up the expressive elements of theatre and creating a Bachelardian activation of my spatial imagination. From the hauntingly focused, austere first reveal of the Skriker to the final sequence when Lily returns from the underworld and it is as if she has been landed on an alien planet, the show surfeited the senses with visual and kinesthetic input in this spatial superimposition of aspects of the world and underworld. There was something interiorized about being taken into the experience of the two human girls, such that the representation of Lily and Josie's social roles, psyches and reproductive histories felt hard to look at directly. Because of that displaced gaze, I could understand the fairy world as a type of exteriorized, mythic manifestation of these intimacies. Yet the fairy world also had its own materiality, and the danced co-presence during every bit of the play's action moved my perception inside and outside of shapes, structures and timelines. The treatment of space and time in *The Skriker* stems from a mode of playwriting that not only thematizes but concretizes a spatial imaginary built of the relationship of inside and outside, nesting and shape-shifting.

Human World/Underworld

The Skriker depicts urban, contemporary London in the 1990s: its human world is a world of council estates and the National Health Service, high-flying capitalism and homeless women begging on the streets. The play posits that

[13] I saw the production of *The Skriker* at the NT between January and March 1994 and watched the NT's archival video of the performance in 2013. Discussion and description of the staging is based on my memory, archival photos and the archival video. Archive file numbers: Rehearsal photos RNT/PP/5/277; Production photos RNT/PR/3/425.

a mostly unseen fairy world exists in complete temporal and spatial concurrence with that world, moving in parallel to human activities and sometimes interacting with them, both maliciously and beneficially. The inhabitants of the fairy world are referred to by Churchill as sprites, fairies or monsters at different times in the script. Smart gave the show a design of boxes within boxes that stirred associations about containment, organization and escape. The world features different locales: there are rooms and parks, interior settings and exterior streets. The underworld seems like a type of no-place, perhaps at most it is a courtyard and a forest. In the characters' perception, the underworld can look like opulence, but it is made of earth and dirt and blood. To go there was to be underground, almost buried, inside and outside suspended together.

There are plentiful pictures of *The Skriker* in the National Theatre's archive. Many of them show the Skriker's intricate incarnations close up, or document the costumes of the Kelpie, Black Annis, Rawheadandbloodybones and other folkloric creatures, such as the Spriggan seen in Figure 1. One picture printed with newspaper reviews suggests the balance of sparseness and boldness in the

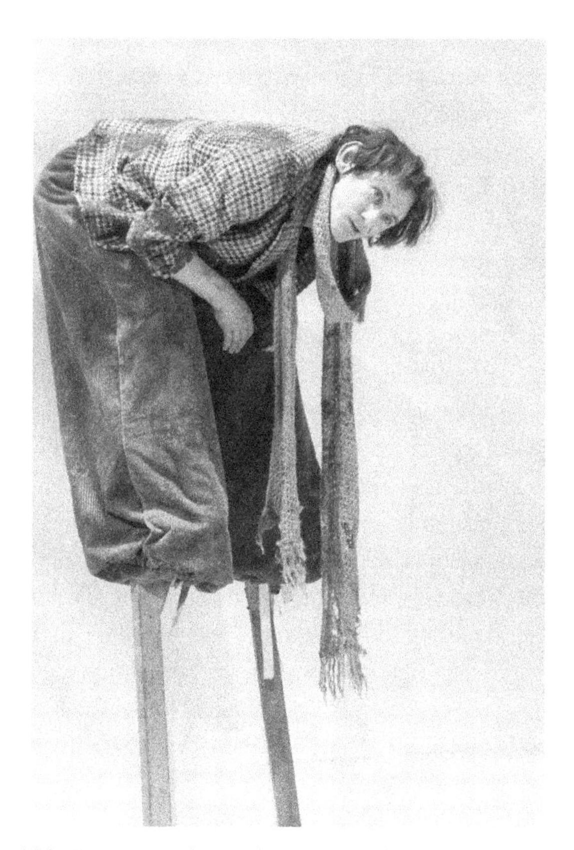

Figure 1 Robbie Barnett as the Spriggan, on stilts. Photo by Hugo Glendinning

stage picture. The photo shows the two nested white boxes that made the center of the set. The larger box was fixed, the smaller box could move forward and back. In the photo, the small box is pushed back, all the way inside the larger box, its front edge flush with the edges of the larger box surrounding it, making a recessed area in the façade. The inner box could also roll forward and because of that, fairy creatures could be on the roof or sides of a "room" in a range of compositions. Some actors could be inside the boxes, or above them, while others were outside or in the center, and this created the multivalent spatiality that conveyed how the daily human world is constantly shared by fairies and sprites and monsters. This set design engages in dialogue with the scenographic aspects of Churchill's playwriting.

Doors in the back and the side of the boxes allowed for other in and out movements. In the newspaper photo, Kathryn Hunter crouches in the Skriker's first incarnation as a death portent. Around her on the floor are rocks maybe the size of ostrich eggs, giving weight to the ground and containing the perimeter of her space, suggesting a fairy circle. The Skriker and the stones look quite irregular against the geometric boxes and Hunter folds her legs and arms around herself in an evocative organic form. Her right arm wraps behind her back at the shoulder, making it look like she has no arm on that side. She wears a bodysuit mishmash of black bandages and on her head sits a terrifying skullcap with spikes of hair extending from it. Behind her, barely seen, moth-y black wings lie on the floor, their ribbing visible in the picture. The picture shows how a contrast of moveable, vertical lines and curvilinear human-scale grotesquerie conjoin human world and fairy world for the play's exploration of mental illness, motherhood and mortality.

In performance, though the two realities are always operative, the Skriker was the only fairy to consistently interact with human beings, and the underworld is only the location in two passages. The rest of the time the fairies played out parallel sequences alongside Lily and Josie in the human world. Lily and Josie are the only two non-fairy characters in the show, producing the sensation that the human population is sparse and that fairies swarm unseen at all times. This created side trajectories without dialogue alongside the main action of the central characters, like and quest of the Bucket-and-Cloth-man to find the right place to spread his cloth and set his bucket of water down, or juxtapositions like Thrumpins riding on the backs of human businessmen with the besuited financiers talking on their cell phones in pursuit of a deal and the Thrumpins mimicking them (Churchill, 1998: 275). Yet the fairies are marginalized in the human world, for all their uncanny resonance. Rarely did any fairy creatures besides the Skriker touch, menace or help the human characters, though they did watch the girls. Nor were they visible to Lily and Josie. Even the Skriker cannot carry out all her desired actions in human reality, though she interacts with the girls in different guises, makes them feel cold and can give them gifts or punishments. Under her thrall, however, Josie murders people so the chaotic, dying energy produced by her homicides will sustain the Skriker. The Skriker exerts power, but cannot simply carry out murder on her own.

The staging got its propulsion from the superimposition of inner and outer dimensions of human and more-than-human spaces. The first production established how *The Skriker* is built out of shape-shifting, its scenography shifting between inside and outside of houses, inside and outside boxes and bodies, inside and outside of life and death (Gobert, 2014: 28). Pregnancy and childbirth, the fundamental given circumstances facing Lily and Josie, are types of shape-shifting, the baby inside and coming out, the mother outside and turned inside out. These are movements on the threshold of life and death. The Skriker cannot seem to die, but Josie's baby died, and Lily discovers she might do anything to protect her baby. As a nonhuman shape-shifter, the Skriker appears in fifteen different guises, transforming sixteen or seventeen times across the course of the play. She reappears in her essential being as a death portent at the top of the show, in the middle and at the end. In the text and the performance, the overlap of the human and fairy world is both an interior reality reflecting Lily and Josie's postpartum perceptions and an exterior reality that is materially happening. The other reality is always waiting to be discovered or emerge from underneath or beside normal perception. The play's unsettling psychological landscape, therefore, amplifies how the boxes of the production design opened like secret spaces and showed things that can't usually be seen.

There are no scene numbers or titles in *The Skriker* text, so all the action flows seamlessly from one moment to the next without intermission; and that unbroken time-flow holds the shape-shifting, superimposed spatiality of the play together. This is most apparent in what happens when the Skriker takes Josie, and then later Lily, to the underworld. The two girls have different experiences of what happens to them in space and time when they agree to go with the Skriker. Josie experiences hundreds of years of captivity in the underworld with the Skriker but returns to the same moment she left, so the temporal experience of eternity in an instant operates on her. When Lily makes what she thinks will be the same bargain and goes with the Skriker to the underworld, she returns not to the moment in time she agreed to go with the Skriker, but to a point in time a century in the future. There, she encounters her granddaughter and deformed great grandchild. This is not a vision of the future, but an actuality she's been hurtled to as if through a wormhole because *The Skriker* taps into the curvilinear shape-shifting properties of the universe and not just the time-bound linear progression of lifecycle existence. The depiction of that future time/place in the stage design was accomplished by dotting larger rocks across the stage. Lily's descendants held a picnic on what seemed like a lunar landscape: the interconnected boxes and shell-like spaces of secrets and revelations blasted open and made barren. This type of spatiotemporal distortion scenographically distilled Churchill's linguistic playfulness and invention on the page and the shattering perceptual shifts created by the show on the stage.

Shape-shifting Language

In *The Skriker*, fractured and allusive language amplifies the spatiotemporal superimposition that drives the show. The Skriker's way of speaking is as dense and tangential as any postmodern word collage but also has the highly referential quality of T. S. Eliot's high modernist poetry. The play begins with a demanding monologue where myth and daily life slam together, and, as they do, the collision causes language to fall apart. One phrase conjures an alliteration that turns into another reference that becomes a malaprop-driven start of a well-known aphorism. Or, a familiar phrase joins with something totally different and creates a horrific or comic juxtaposition. "May day, she cries, may pole axed me to help her. So I spin the sheaves shoves shivers into golden guild and geld," explains the Skriker. The Skriker comments on her own shape-shifting in passages like "I've been a hairy here he is changeling changing chainsaw massacre a sieve to carry water from the well well what's to be done? Brother brewed beer in an eggshell. I said I'm old old every so olden dazed but I never see saw marjory before three two one blast off!" (243–4). The language creates a sense of repetition and terror. Then, along with the spatial shift to the underworld, the spoken language shifts to song and continues the intensification of the production's phenomenological impact.

In performance, Hunter's technique mattered a great deal to the language's impact. As the Skriker's opening monologue spun its tale (Rumpelstiltskin is one of the monologue's central references), Hunter from time to time unfurled the wings on her costume. Hunter's emotional and vocal intensity and physical flexibility were central to the first production's success with staging shape-shifting. Smart remembers Hunter and Churchill working through the opening monologue together tirelessly and how much she admired Hunter because the actress insisted on understanding the text, image by image, rather than just "doing it on the music" of the words.[14] In other words, the associative logic of the fractured language mattered to Hunter, she invested in linking the images to the Skriker's action, rather than just performing the words automatically, or

[14] Sara Freeman, Interview with Les Waters and Annie Smart, Berkeley, California, January 30, 2010. Taped interview; Transcribed.

using them to create emotional flow without knowing why the language worked this way on the imagination.

This dizzying four-page monologue presents a specific type of scenographic challenge. Textually and linguistically, its job is not simply to productively baffle the senses. In terms of plot, it directly functions as a prologue that foreshadows all the events of the play. Though that is primarily visible to the audience only in retrospect, still the Skriker must speak with purpose. The Skriker knows the story she's telling has already happened, or is always already happening. Visually, it could be very static, though in part because the Skriker is such an arresting character, it did not feel static even though she does not shift shape during it. In the archival video, I was surprised to discover that Hunter speaks much more slowly than I remembered. The monologue felt fast when I watched it live. By contrast, the songs in the underworld are lurid and onomatopoetic but far less difficult to understand. "Welcome homesick/drink drank drunk" begins the spirits' song as Josie arrives in the underworld. "Avocado and prawn cockfight cockup cocksuck," the spirits gleefully sing. This type of wordplay about the feast they serve is interspersed with very direct warnings from the spirit of another girl imprisoned in the underworld. The girl bursts in "Don't eat. It's glamour. It's blood and dirty water Don't eat, don't drink or you'll never get back" (269–70). The language paradoxically becomes more direct in the underworld as the musical setting becomes more complex. Josie and Lily's senses are deeply befuddled by their transport, so it is just as much work for them to figure out what to do or not do in the underworld as it was for them to assess how to interact with the Skriker in their world. And the audience experiences the same thing. The playful, fractured language registers how deeply challenged Lily and Josie's perception is and at the same time challenges audience perception.

In performance, Hunter gloried in the underworld induction sequence, dressed in gold lame and savoring the song. But later in the underworld, the Skriker returns to her form as a death portent, wrapped in black and contorted as pictured in Figure 2, and her dialogue with Josie explains how terrible contemporary human beings taste as compared to those in the past. This scene contains a monologue that is not as long as the opening one but is otherwise its complete partner in linguistic complexity and spatial superimposition, troubling its function as exposition in a way that is both playful and sinister. This monologue contains phrases that encapsulate the play's perspective on environmental degradation in the contemporary world because of pollution and ozone thinning, such as when the Skriker describes people as tasting as if they come from a "toxic waste paper basket case" or have "salmonelephantiasis." She says they

Figure 2 Close up of Kathryn Hunter as the Skriker in death portent form. Photo by Hugo Glendinning

are "dry as dustpans, foul as shitpandemonium" because of "Poison in the food chainsaw massacre" (274–5).

The key thing about this sequence is that Josie now understands the Skriker better; she can hear and read the meaning in the jumble of words, references and images and because of that, she starts to negotiate. She proposes that the Skriker take her back up to the human world so they can look for more human sustenance. When the Skriker refuses, Josie hears the emptiness in the monster's threat. Josie no longer believes the Skriker's warning about the water in the fountain. She plunges her hands into the water. Josie has been told she will die if she does so, but instead, she transports back to the human world at exactly the moment she left it.

In her transports, Josie is like a reverse Persephone: she goes to the underworld because of a longing but also to protect Lily by taking the Skriker's torment from her. She is returned to the human world not by loving intervention but because of her willingness to risk death. When she returns to the human world, her perception is heightened, her sight and her sense of smell made acute because of deprivation, and her expectation of death makes her especially vulnerable to Lily's gentleness:

JOSIE	Too bright. No it's bright there. My eyes don't work. Hold me.
LILY	Now what?
JOSIE	You smell like people. Your hair smells like hair. It was like putting a gun to my head because they always said I'd die if I did that. Liars, you hear me? I got away. Yah. Can't get me.
LILY	Stop it. You can stop it.
JOSIE	I was ready to die. I thought I'd never get back. (275)

Lily hugs Josie at the end of this exchange, after establishing that what she has experienced is a normal day of going to the shops and meeting a child in the park and that she, Lily, is tired because she's very, very pregnant. Josie's jarring experience of being in both worlds is distilled in the contrast between the Skriker's disintegrated language and Lily's prosaic language. Josie's shifting perception is one of many instances in the play where intense moments of consciousness accompany Lily and Josie's interactions with the Skriker.

Seeing the Self and Changing the Self

Throughout the production, both higher tech and lower tech means amplified the phenomenological sense of consciousness perceiving itself in the spatiotemporal constructs of the text and staging. Virtuosic extensions of the human body, fast changes and abstract movement defined the moments of recognition where Lily and Josie see the Skriker for what she is and name her effects on them. The play's repeated interplay of transformation and recognition demonstrates the consistent use of spatial superimpositions where layered visual effects or improbable physical juxtapositions pinpoint the moment and experience of perception. In *The Skriker*, this often occurs as a displacement between when the audience understands the Skriker to be present and when Lily and Josie recognize her.

In Waters's staging and Ian Spink's choreography, the Skriker often emerged from under or beside things, like in the moment when her head pokes through the cushion of a couch where Josie and Lily are sitting (see Figure 3). After speaking to them, she steps out of the couch dressed as a sort of ballerina/fairy princess/pink fairy in a tutu and with wings (262–3). But just as often, Hunter would simply step into the frame of the boxes, smoothly, almost imperceptibly, in a new guise as an American businesswoman, or a homeless beggar, or someone who claimed to once have been Lily and Josie's school friend. In either type of "arrival," the audience could understand that the Skriker was there in a new iteration before the characters did, though Hunter's disappearance into the new

Figure 3 Kathryn Hunter as the Skriker, Jacqueline Defferary as Lily and Sandy McDade as Josie. Photo by Hugo Glendinning

guises fooled me once or twice. When the *characters* apprehended the Skriker, their behavior changed and consciousness jolted, prompting a new sensation of the moment and the self in the moment. In the text, this type of reveal and recognition gets iterated each time the script describes a new character and then states "it is the SKRIKER." That tag appears ten times in the script and has a hypnotic or ritual ring to it, the all caps convention for character names making it seem even more emphatic. The text tells the reader "it is the Skriker" but Josie and Lily don't realize until a later moment, and in performance the audience always has the option or foreknowledge to see it before them. This is a moment of the space "crossing the image," a dynamic Patrice Pavis identifies where the staging of a moment allows for a reading of the image in space in a way that cannot quite be conveyed by the inscription in the text (2013: 63–75).

These moments of seeing the Skriker preface what is perhaps the most intellectually challenging and emotionally terrifying sequence of *The Skriker*, a scene that wrestles with the impact of an ontologically troubling experience of self-perception for Josie. Three-quarters of the way through the play Lily is taking care of her infant daughter and hosting Josie, who is visiting while she prepares dinner. Josie is under the Skriker's thrall, committing murder to keep the Skriker fed and behaving horribly toward the baby because she is jealous of the attention Lily gives it. Lily, angry at Josie's callousness to her daughter, wishes for Josie not to be crazy. With a snap, the Skriker grants Lily's wish, and takes away her glamour on Josie. This produces Josie's only moment of recognition about what she did to her own baby. Instantly, with the Skriker's snap, Josie "hurts." For a moment, Josie reacts with real knowledge and pain about killing her baby:

> I killed her. Did I? Yes. I hadn't forgotten but. She was just as precious. Yours isn't the only. If I hadn't she'd still. I keep knowing it again, what can I do? Why did I? It should have been me. Because under the pain oh shit there's under that there's this other/under that there's. (279)

Josie's language also falls apart here and repeats itself. Her culpability and self-assessment in this moment terrifies both girls. Lily "wishes her back," and Josie instantly returns to her previous demeanor, dismissive about the baby and obsessed with proving to Lily that she was taken to the fairy underworld. This is a truly difficult passage in the play because a moment of recognition like this should allow the main characters to take a new decision or start a new action, but that does not happen. It is a *coup de theatre* that closes in on itself, inside and outside converging. As a representation of the psyche, and as a phenomenological occasion in theatre, this fairy story is repetitive and reflexive, not redemptive or linear.

This scene holds the tragic insight of *The Skriker* and its terror reveals that our powers of recognition can be permanently altered by trauma and transformation. The scene therefore begins with Lily talking about how your perception changes when you have a baby: "I can't help it," says Lily. "Everything's shifted around so she's in the middle. I never minded things. But everything dangerous seems it might get her" (276–7). As a spatiotemporal construct, *The Skriker* is both a memory house about the inside/outside experience of maternity and a social map about the superimposed experience of disenfranchisement and danger.

Feminist Theatre, Political Theatre, Physical Theatre

As a text and an event in space, *The Skriker* is a construct that combines a heterogeneous range of styles, moves beyond dialogue and emphasizes the materiality of the performer. Consider again the feast scene: dance, song and dialogue accompany Josie's arrival in the underworld. In Waters and Smart's production, the stage picture was sculpted out of the bodies of performers who then broke apart as if the fairies were a swarm of insects: in that moment, I couldn't decode the lyrics of the song fast enough to be sure of the what they said, yet my skin crawled. Hunter's incarnation in a gold lame gown and her powerful stance as she sang with gusto traded on a dual perception of her as "Kathryn Hunter" and the Skriker at the same time. The Pina Bausch-esque assemblage of things happening throughout the show put the audience both inside and outside the story, inside and outside the text, and inside and outside the moment in time and space. At the end of the play, when the Passerby stopped dancing and the stage went dark, I remember feeling unsure if I had been sucked into a black hole or expelled from one.

Churchill's established power as a feminist and political dramatist join in this play with cross-over forms of physical and visual theatre. The result is writing that can be fully experimental and spatial in lodging its social critiques. *The Skriker* conveys the phenomenological experiences of teenage motherhood, the economic disenfranchisement of working-class youth and the social demands of gender performance. It is especially strong on gendered issues related to insanity and violence because mind–body dualism carries extra judgment for women and the abject of society. The play's content also links its characters – human and non-human – to the state of ecological crisis that human activity has created and brought to a breaking point in the twenty-first century. In this, Churchill's theatre-making connects to the way that ecodramatic investigations and dramaturgical structures rise in twenty-first-century playwriting as part of feminist and political analyses and aesthetic innovation.

The Skriker's bridging of the theatre of text and the theatre of image in these scenographic ways figures as a feminist act: an act that recovers the body – so often denigrated as feminine and fallen as compared to the elevated masculine mind in traditional gender dualities – and transposes it into text-based theatre. *The Skriker* is, in its way, a type of state-of-the-nation play though it was not recognized in its time as such because of the centering of young women, the attention to the psychophysical interconnectedness of identity and its sense that the balance of natural world matters as much to society as the state of Parliament. Part of what *The Skriker* heralds for contemporary playwriting is a sophisticated reactivation of feminist and political theatre trajectories, realized with arresting spatiality to register critique in ways visceral, visual and verbal. With its melding of the properties of text-based feminist theatre and cross-over physical forms, *The Skriker* uses bodies in space in a way that reroutes "paradox of physical theatre," a paradox about how the liberation of the actor's body and gesture does not instantaneously undo the forces of authority in staging and meaning-creation (Pavis, 2013: 181). Even when a performance is created without or before a written text, and even when it comes from the impulses of the body of the performer, it will not achieve a state of unmediated being; it will be theatricalized. A spatial reading of *The Skriker* affirms how its writing and storytelling is not an authorial endeavor that undermines the sophistication of the body-based work: it is innovative playwriting that values the scenographic interplay of interior and exterior and activates the spatial imagination.

3 Naomi Iizuka: Simultaneity and Permeability

At the Vanishing Point employs a spatial simultaneity that makes the past and present coincident and synchronous; it is a spatiotemporal construction that makes it seem like there is a before and after, an in-front of and a behind, but there is really only one concurrence. It is a show Naomi Iizuka has premiered twice. Her rise to prominence as a playwright came in part because of productions at Actors Theater of Louisville's Humana Festival of New American Plays. In the run-up to the 2004 festival, Amy Wegener, ATL's literary manager and dramaturg, invited her to engage in a process of collaborative creation with Les Waters, not just submit a script. The result was a site-based warehouse performance inspired by the history of one Louisville's neighborhoods: people who lived there, types of businesses located there, political events and natural disasters that impacted the area. *At the Vanishing Point* impressionistically conveys more than a century of history about the Butchertown neighborhood, with particular focus on the meatpacking Henzel family and the photographer Ralph Eugene Meatyard.

Iizuka's return to the show in 2015 made the play's pitch more metaphysical than documentary, but no less formally experimental. The text changed between the two incarnations, yet its structure as a sequence of monologues remained and its themes about emplacement still resonated strongly. It is a play built around themes of love, perception, knowledge and memory spatialized in such a way as to connect the humble, broken-down or forgotten spaces in Butchertown to the immensity of the universe's patterns. The play exhibits Iizuka's methods of fracturing or abandoning naturalist plot development, embracing time-bending overlapping sequences and folding together erudition, intense imagery and multi-vocal perspectives on history.

At the Vanishing Point emphasizes personal reminiscence and local geography; Iizuka's writing allows any sort of plot, which it does not precisely mandate, to emerge as a function of events sharing a space in the theatre, in Butchertown and Louisville. The expressive elements of theatre reorganize more toward being a landscape, in the sense Gertrude Stein theorized. Iizuka indeed renders text on the page without capitalization and with a strong sense of the rhythmic breaks and elisions in everyday speech in a way that decenters subjectivity and produces a seemingly stream-of-consciousness prose reminiscent of Stein. But there's something phenomenologically Steinian about it too. This show, in both incarnations, synthesized aspects of modernist experiments with time and language and postmodern approaches to technology and history. Watching it created a sense of time travel in me. At the premiere of the revised show in 2015, a shimmering synchronicity seemed to fill the air of the theatre. I ended up abandoning myself to a sense of floating: it felt like the memories of

Figure 4 Bruce McKenzie in *At the Vanishing Point* at Actors Theatre of Louisville. Photo by Bill Brymer

Louisville being shared on stage had become my memories, while, at best, I had only strolled through Butchertown once or twice while visiting.

Both times I watched the show, I felt an intimacy with the performers, but also perceived the totality of the stage picture as if looking into a telescope in order to see a whole world. The performers didn't honor any fourth wall division between stage and auditorium. Every character spoke directly to the audience; so much so that Bruce McKenzie's performance as the Photographer initially felt unscripted, his casual body language, his offhand delivery and the way he was known to audiences at Humana from his appearances in other shows in previous years combining to make him familiar, almost a beloved school teacher figure as seen in Figure 4. The stories accumulated into a structure defined by place and stillness rather than linear time and action: the river, the architecture and the roads of Louisville were the underpinnings of the show's treatment of time and space. The show's scenographic combination of history and the present made a Bachelardian intimate immensity, a memory house mapped on to the city.

History and/as the Present

At the Vanishing Point participates in an open-ended aesthetics of presence: there is no description of time and setting that prefaces the play. The play begins with the Photographer, based on Meatyard, saying "i want to show you something."[15] The moment is now. He wants to show slides from an old-style slide cartridge projected on a portable screen. They are pictures that upend simple perception. Yet what gets shown, inexorably, as the show unfolds, is the past – moments from the speakers' lives and events that impacted the city. Personal histories join civic histories. As these histories are conjured, they are present again, but the status of the speaker wobbles in the representation. Iizuka's play provides a series of portraits of actual people who lived and moved in Louisville's landscape, laboring, making meaning and making art. The links between the people are attenuated – it is not a direct genealogical line that connects them, though the stories they tell fill in connections between them as they reference fathers or cousins, uncles or wives, work colleagues and siblings.

The play has two parts rather than a series of acts and scenes: part one is labeled "self portrait," and it is made up of a ten-page monologue by the Photographer, who is an artist but also works as an optometrist to support his family. Part two bears the heading "snapshots from a family album." For the most part, the audience is not seeing vignettes that are happening *as if* in the times the characters are talking about. They are watching the people remember. The characters on stage are all based on real people. Some were interviewed by Iizuka, some recovered from historical research, and, in the musician Ben Sollee's case in 2015, one was actually being himself as he spoke. All the people depicted are in the same moment as the audience and, as they remember the past, history is there, simultaneously. Two realities are happening as the characters talk. What is shown is the process of remembering, of materializing the past and dematerializing the present, and vice versa, in a spatial simultaneity.

In 2015, Iizuka and Waters went back to the 2004 text, adding and deleting material to create a tighter arc. They also invited Lexington-born cellist Sollee to collaborate on the show. Sollee both accompanied the show live and delivered a newly crafted monologue. In the show's modified documentary style, his monologue autobiographically told of his heritage and life in Kentucky while thematizing the connectedness of all the intimate family snapshots, old technologies and bits of artistic creation referred to in the play. These are invoked as tokens and memories that are part of a vast universe in which human life takes on its vibration and meaning. With the cuts and additions (three monologues removed; one added), the show somehow got more specific and at the same time bigger.

[15] All lack of capitalizations in quotations and rendering of punctuation reflect Iizuka's practice.

In the modified proscenium space of the Pamela Brown auditorium, designer Annie Smart created a monumental but simple set for the play's unfolding. It had a stunningly angled metallic back wall with sliding doors in it, an "edifice" which reviewer Todd Zeigler rightly links to the "aging industrial character" of Butchertown, Louisville's former meatpacking district (2015). The space featured a raked forestage, a scrim of the sunset sky and a sweep of grass invoking the Kentucky countryside. Light effects dilated the focus on the set inward and outward, and video projections were used especially when depicting the storm that in 1937 caused the Ohio River to flood. There was a strong interplay between the metal solidity of the back wall and the evanescence of light.

Pictures of the show record panoramas of Smart's landscape or close ups on individual actors. In pictures, there is often a central figure talking and chiaroscuro behind them, or two figures separated and highlighted. In the staging, the simultaneity of past and present in the play's space of memory juxtaposed the speaker of the monologue with another figure on stage, a ghost or some embodied co-presence of a memory. The ghosts, as much as the telling of history, spatialize the two realities of the play: the play is a metastasized history play as well as a pluralized memory play with past and present, always on each other's horizon.

There is a sequence in the play, however, where all the memories and all the researched history burst forth at the same time as if it is happening on stage at that moment and make a whirlpool or tornado of images that now *happen* in action on stage, not just in memory: history and/as the present. The scenography at this moment deployed light effects, sound, projections and the movement of the doors in the metal facade to create the storm of 1937 and the fires of 1855. As also discussed in Section 1, at that moment the text's stage directions suggest a torrent of activity focused on a boy in old-fashioned clothes and a girl in a white dress running through the shadows in the space while we hear the sound of children whispering. Iizuka indicates that the whispers should be a "susurration of historical facts underneath everything," such as

> linden hill was built in 1815. bourbon stockyards were established in 1834. the kentucky distillery company burned to the ground august 14, 1890. the school for the blind was established in 1842. woodland gardens were opened in 1828. the german american civic school opened in 1865. (24–5)

In performance, it felt as if a crack in the space–time continuum had opened and momentarily ruptured, with multiple characters contending for attention at once.

It is possible to be precise about time in the play with retrospective analysis; each successive monologue telescopes back from the 1970s and 1960s to the

1930s and the teens, back all the way to the 1850s and earlier, until the storm, after which the characters' monologues start moving toward the present again, returning toward the Photographer. At the juncture of the storm, the past asserts itself and history speaks directly. Interestingly, a loop back to the Photographer happens without re-centering his voice: it is not a full circle, it is a shifted lens – in Frank Henzel's monologue, the penultimate one, the Photographer's memories get conveyed from another perspective and those memories are displaced and replaced in the eighth and final monologue delivered by the Photographer's sister-in-law Maudie Totten.

And then there is the way the masked and ghostly presences of children heighten the simultaneity of history and the present. The 2015 production used three child actors who appeared in different tableaux representing, variously, the Meatyard children, the Henzel cousins as children and the children killed or displaced in various Louisville disasters. A child first appears when the Photographer talks about learning to take photographs because he wanted to take pictures when his first son was born: "i loved him very much and i wanted, i wanted to understand what i was seeing when i looked at him" (6–8). Gradually, each of the Photographer's three children is revealed as he talks: in the production sliding doors opened to reveal them behind the Photographer in an upper-level opening in the rust-colored back wall. Later in part one, we see the Photographer's wife haunt the stage the same way, wearing an uncanny mask, as he speaks about a series of photos he made of his children in derelict buildings and his family in masks from the "five and dime."

The uncanniness I experienced from the wife and, later, the children appearing in the background tableaux in masks, as seen in Figure 5, created the sense of haunting. In part two, the family album, the children also appear in period clothing to embody a girl who might be the young woman Nora Holtz's father loved and Martin Kinflein's father. Two of the children are also the Boy and the Girl who speak and move during the storm sequence, as if they are the very embodiment of the neighborhood, and they are also an indication of the social violence visited on children and the dispossessed in history in this location. When these children appear, they stand affixed in a space, and then sometimes burst into movement. Always in the text children are associated with images of birds, which in the production was accomplished through projections and sound effects.

The children's final appearance is as Pete and Fred Henzel and Ronnie Marston, their cousin, in Halloween masks that echo the Photographer's use of masks. This emphasizes how in every appearance, the children's presence is a surrogacy for other previously invoked memories, linking history and the present. One striking photograph of the show captures a moment when the

Figure 5 Dan Waller, Brandon Greenwald and Gabe Wieble in *At the Vanishing Point* at Actors Theatre of Louisville. Photo by Bill Brymer

Figure 6 Ava Johnson and Brandon Greenwald in *At the Vanishing Point* at Actors Theatre of Louisville. Photo by Bill Brymer

children are representing ghosts of children killed in the 1937 flood, standing stage right, just before starting to run in long-looping circles around the center of the stage, for a moment statues in a natural landscape (see Figure 6). The children are an embodiment of the past come to life, and an expression of the energy of memory and storytelling in stillness and then in motion. This type of spatiotemporal blur and focus scenographically sets up the play's arrival at and reflection on the vanishing point where life and death converge.

Blurring and Focusing Language

Caridad Svich writes of Iizuka as a "poet of the hybrid," and develops the frame of "polyglot Latino theatre" for describing the culture-crossing, decomposing and recomposing use of language seen in writers like Iizuka (Svich, 2006: 195). Here it is interesting to think about how *At the Vanishing Point* provides an engagement with the white, working-class history of Louisville's Butchertown neighborhood and yet also expresses insights central to the artistic perspective of a Latina-Asian-American dramatist who treats language like a modernist poet and form like a postmodern flaneur. In *At the Vanishing Point*, Iizuka uses language to create the effect of simultaneous blurring and focus that she positions as the central perceptual activity of memory. In this, she marries looking and speaking, using words to open up spatial perception and compliment what both photography and scenography can do in making people look again and perceive anew.

The monologues in *At the Vanishing Point* are types of personal history, both poetic distillations and constructions of witness, as discussed in the section below on documentary theatre. But it is also true that some of the speeches are embedded expository lectures, a tactic Iizuka deploys in other shows where she often has characters who are academics, or some form of "experts in their fields" discourse on a subject (Wren, 2002). *Vanishing Point* begins with the Photographer's speech, in which he instructs the audience about both the art of looking, the way an eye perceives, and the art of listening, that is, how to understand jazz and other types of experimental music.

The real Meatyard experimented with extreme close-up, with blurring, with overlap and with photographing masked figures; he also worked as an optician. Iizuka's Photographer therefore shows a blurry image on a portable projection screen and explains the physiology of how the eye selects and arranges things in order to focus perception. He conveys how "your brain takes all your experience and knowledge of the world, and it forms a kind of context by which to process and make sense of that information." He elaborates an example:

> so that say you're standing in the middle of a field, and you hold up your hand in front of your eyes and everything else, the field and beyond, it becomes a blur, and all you see are the particulars of your own hand, the lines

> embedded in your palm, the whorls and ridges of your fingertips or the feel of your wife's hair warm from the sun, all of these things, more, and so you understand what it is you're seeing because of all the associations and memories of a whole lifetime. (1–2)

The Photographer's words evoke rich sensual detail, mobilizing language to produce feeling in an audience, who will imagine and remember the sensations of sun, the baseball glove, their own skin.

The effect of imagining or remembering those sensations as he speaks heightens the sense of intimacy. Then Iizuka switches approaches, and has the Photographer turn attention to how we can shift our perception from the intimate detail to the full immensity even in the same moment:

> let's say you shift your gaze to what lies beyond your hand, and so the frame, it changes, and what was a blur is now clear and distinct. and what you see is a field, and in the distance, a human figure slowly walking away from you, towards a point far in the distance, a point beyond the horizon line, beyond where you can see . (2)

The play's language bursts with sensory details while considering things almost too abstract to be conceptualized, like love and death. Many of the monologues describe nature, or speak of sounds, the feel of wind or air, the ravages of fire and the jolt of electricity, the smell of earth and blood. Iizuka's language creates the sensation of blur and focus we can experience with our eyes as well as our ears.

This visual–aural quality of language means the play's collection of monologues are not only an account of history but also a choral poem. Meatyard thought photography was most closely allied with poetry: words are pictures; the relationship between how language shifts perception and how pictures shift perception is closely linked, as part of a profound self-reflective encounter with consciousness. Iizuka's lack of capitalization can also be read as being about the role of the perceiving the self; by denying a reader and speaker the visual "lifting up" or marking usually associated with proper nouns, nouns of the self, she is shifting seeing and understanding, placing the self in a more contingent, dissolved, plural space.

In performance, the way McKenzie as the Photographer recounted the experience of fitting a young man with new glasses embodied the sensation of blurring into focus Iizuka activates in the text. This sense of blur and clarity is a type of simultaneity and Iizuka's sequencing creates a time-bending payoff of recognition. Early in his monologue, the Photographer describes how a young man came into his shop. The Photographer realizes his new patient has severe astigmatism and had never seen the world unblurred before. After giving him the glasses, the Photographer says the young man "said he never saw so clearly in his life. he said it hurt to see everything so sharp and clear. to be that aware was almost too much, it was almost too much to bear" (3–4). This crystalline language about clear sight being too much to bear comes back at the end of Frank Henzel's monologue, when he tells the same story in a way that reveals that the young man was Jimmy, his cousin Ronnie's husband, and that Jimmy was about to ship out to Vietnam, where he died. Jimmy's death widows Ronnie, information shared in her monologue earlier in the show. In that stage moment, Jimmy, Ronnie, Frank and the Photographer are at last in the same place together as part of the play's spatialization of consciousness, a recognition at the vanishing point.

The Vanishing Point

In photography, vanishing point perspective creates a sense of depth, an illusion of convergence in the distance. One Louisville reviewer of Iizuka's show wondered if the vanishing point might be "something more than a visual abstraction," in a way that speaks to how Iizuka's scenographic writing invites a postmodern, self-reflective activation of consciousness. What if the vanishing point were "a physical place," wrote Marty Rosen. "Or, what if the vanishing point isn't visual at all, but a central idea or thesis that flits around the periphery of our consciousness, only to disappear when we try to focus on it?" (2015). In the text and on the stage, Iizuka's play repeatedly invokes consciousness at the vanishing point: first, the show depicts a return to consciousness through really looking, as represented by the Photographer's passages quoted above. Then there's an extension of consciousness beyond the realm of the human perception of life or death, as found in Pete Henzel's way of confronting grief. Finally, there's a savoring of consciousness as described by Maudie Totten at the end of the play.

Pete Henzel's reflections on talking to the dead echoed across the stage as he confronted his grief, unleashing the narratives of the other speakers. Pete works as a tour guide in the Louisville house where Thomas Edison lived in 1866 during a stint as a local telegraph operator. Pete knows the history of Edison's efforts to build a thanophone, a machine by which people could talk to the dead. And he believes that consciousness indeed works that way – that the end is not the end – "what i'm talking about, see, is a kind of manifestation of displaced energy and the harnessing of a kind of flow or wave of charged particles of human consciousness," he says. In the production, Pete spoke directly to the audience, the third monologue in the sequence. The opening monologues by the Photographer and Ben Sollee served as a type of invocation, and then Pete set the revelation in motion. After him, each successive monologue talks to the dead more than the one before, moving from Pete's cousin Ronnie who mourns her husband and cousin Frank; to Nora, a girl Pete's uncle Martin loved in his youth; on from her to Martin; and, after the storm, to Frank himself, who Pete claims to have seen by the riverside in a ghostly visitation from beyond the vanishing point.

In the final monologue, by contrast, Maudie's stillness and glow silenced the space again as the play ended. There was no ghost meeting her, just an acknowledgment of all she had seen and done, the epiphany that life could be complete and enough, but never enough, stealing over her. This echoes right back to where the Photographer began: with the acknowledgment that there are things we want to say or show, but we will never be able to convey it all. It is like the pictures of zen twigs the Photographer shows at the beginning of the show and to which Maudie refers at the end. The twig images are part of a series that the real Meatyard created, and his naming them as "zen" speaks to a philosophy, a mysticism and a spirituality the play allows to float over its engagement of consciousness. During Waters's time as artistic director at ATL, he commissioned shows about nature poet Wendell Berry and Christian theologian Thomas Merton, and returned to this show about Meatyard. The three Kentucky mystics were all friends, it turns out, and the sense of existential convergence and disappearance they all investigated in their work pervades *At the Vanishing Point*.

Documentary Theatre, Site-Based Staging and Installation

The metaphysical inquiry that seems to dominate *At the Vanishing Point* shifts the balance of a project that began as a documentary theatre process and a site-based engagement. In truth, the wellspring of *Vanishing Point* was multiple: it included Iizuka and Waters's shared interest in photography, Iizuka's investigations of history from below, her search for mythic patterns and resonances and her connection to Louisville from numerous periods of festival residency there. The documentary research, interviews and experiential encounters with a neighborhood that fertilized the play situates *Vanishing Point* in the revival of documentary forms that marked early twenty-first century, even if Iizuka's way of shaping the play that resulted has nothing to do with the verbatim reproduction of words people said to her or a singular focus on historical events.

In the UK docudrama has been a particular site of revival and experimentation since the 1990s, but in the United States the solo work of Anna Deveare Smith and the ensemble the work of Tectonic Theatre company and The Civilians have also provided an upsurge in the range of ways experimental documentary theatre manifests. Rebellato notes that the resurgence of documentary drama impacted other modes of dramatic expression as well. "A documentary feel crept into other fictional genres," he observes, considering documentary plays that have fictional elements, and, conversely, fictional plays that use strategies like lecture-demonstrations and the projection of statistics or timelines associated with documentary theatre. "The general impression of this type of work is that in the twenty-first century," he writes, "we have preferred our fiction to be dressed up as documentary" (Rebellato, 2013: 13).

Related to Iizuka's experimentation with the conventions of documentary and site-based forms, Sean Metzger makes the useful argument that *Vanishing Point* represents an aspect of the "Asian/American critique" in Iizuka's work even though its subjects are not directly related to Asian-American identity. For Metzger, the notion of Asian/American critique draws together an analysis across space, time and bodies to effect a "subjectless" critical operation that displaces "logics of racial exclusion" or "racial essentialism" (Metzger, 2011: 278–9). In other words, for Metzger, Iizuka's theatre is powerful because it presents identity as part of a set of situated relationships and treats racial formation within these matrices. Metzger makes clear that the subject matter of *At the Vanishing Point* is not not-racialized in its whiteness; it takes on whiteness in its specificity in Louisville with a site-based staging. In 2015, the show was no longer performed in a warehouse onsite in Butchertown. But was it still site-specific to Louisville, even in ATL's main house? We can think about that question this way: is it conceivable the show would ever be performed in any other city? The way that *At the Vanishing Point* in some ways has to *happen* in Louisville means its remapping of the city turns into something like a happening at a gallery.

Patrice Pavis writes about the techniques of installation and juxtaposition as being useful for not wanting to "explain" content or meaning, but rather to just let it *be* or *emerge* (2013: 201, 305). This is the same theory that underpins the performances of live art, experimental art-performance, happenings and the work of many installation artists – don't explain, just be. Also like much contemporary performance art, technology is central to how meaning emerges through Iizuka's spatiotemporal assemblage. The layering of live and mediatized elements is immediately recognizable as an aesthetic strategy of almost two generations of postmodern performance experimentation, as well as part of the heritage of documentary and epic theatre.

Technology is now absorbed everywhere in theatre and playwrights reflect that in their texts. Sierz observes that

> the effect of new digital media on the theatrical imagination has been to speed up and complicate story-telling, to widen our sense of what is possible on stage and to make our idea of communication more sophisticated. This is expressed in the way playwrights construct narratives, especially in the way these jump from scene to scene and from idea to idea or image to image, and the way they are full of short and, to use an old-tech word, "telegraphic" dialogue. (2011: 10)

While Iizuka doesn't write projections into the text of *At the Vanishing Point*, she certainly sets up her text in ways that jump from image to image, distills the language in telegraphic ways and overlaps time and space as discussed above. She also weaves references to a range of "old" technologies throughout the play as part of reorienting the audience's perception and raising the idea of reaching across time to talk to the dead: there's the Photographer's slide carrell, table-top projector and portable screen, and also his vintage records, played on record player that's only steps away from being a gramophone. Sollee came out with an old tape player and played a cassette, on which we heard his mother sing. How far is this from Edison's thanophone, which Pete speaks about? Ronnie, Frank and Maudie talk about the old type of machinery used in the slaughterhouses. Nora Holtz pins her hopes for independence in the future on the way she is mastering the then-new technology of typing, despite her blindness. Record players, typewriters, audiocassettes, slide projectors: visual and audio technology are part of the scenographic interplay of the intimate interior lives of the characters and immensity of the universe.

The mosaic-like-structure of *At the Vanishing Point*, its spatialized approach to memory, its dignification of working-class voices and its poetic language produced the sensation of a simultaneity on stage that transcends death. This sensation was amplified by reflecting that Waters had recently directed *Our Town* on the ATL mainstage and McKenzie had played the Stage Manager. McKenzie's appearance as the Photographer made another link in the web of associations simultaneously sharing the space, another set of ghosts in the background of the composition. At ATL, *Our Town* set the stage for *At the Vanishing Point,* the mid-century writing of Wilder and its incipient scenographic qualities giving way to the more postdramatic spatiality of Iizuka's play. Likewise, *At the Vanishing Point* in some ways set the stage for Ruhl's *For Peter Pan*, which premiered in the same place just a year later. Ruhl's play layers horizontal and vertical spatial impulses as part of its consideration of life, afterlife and the theatre.

4 Sarah Ruhl: Layering and Flight

Sarah Ruhl's *For Peter Pan on Her 70th Birthday* reworks her mother's family history and presents five adult siblings processing their father's death in the liminal spaces of a hospital room, a wake and a dreamscape, layering their family story with *Peter Pan*, a play the oldest sibling performed in during her youth. The show premiered in Louisville in March of 2016 at the Humana Festival, and the run was a bit rough.[16] The night I saw it, the wires got tangled. Literally. In the third movement, Ann and her siblings, doubling as the characters from a pantomime *Peter Pan*, hooked the flying cables into their harnesses and things immediately went awry. The stage manager came over the mic and called hold. The action stopped. Some of the actors collapsed their posture, irritated. Kathleen Chalfant, playing Ann, looked bemused and pumped her legs, increasing the arc of her swing.

The pause to resolve technical difficulties lasted for what felt like ten minutes. At some point the actors gave up and got jolly despite being suspended in the air. They started telling jokes to each other like the characters do at the wake in movement two. Then they started singing "When the Saints Come Marching In," a reprise from the play's first movement. Chalfant asked the audience if we knew the next verse. Someone started in on it, and we in the audience had a sing-along with the actors. It was like the *Sound of Music* sing-a-longs that had become popular events at theatre venues around the country–a testament to the community theatre forms Ruhl valorizes in *For Peter Pan* and throughout her work when she writes about her mother as a theatre artist. When the show was ready to start again, Chalfant asked the audience if we remembered where they were. Magically, someone in the house cued her. The play resumed, so close to its end but needing its full vertical flying sequence before re-grounding in the epilogue.

That stoppage was a doubling and redoubling of the moments of self-reflective consciousness the play sets up with its spatiotemporal layering. The space of the Pamela Brown Theatre seemed to contract as we sang together and waited through this "out of time" moment. The towering vertical set pieces Annie Smart created for the nursery represented the walls of a room from the perspective of a small child. This nodded to the Bachelardian sensation of how big your house feels when you are young and how it feels too small when you

[16] In addition to Ruhl's play, the roster for the 2016 Humana Festival included *Residence* by Laura Jacqumin, *This Random World* by Steven Dietz, *Wellesley Girl* by Brendan Pelsue, *Cardboard Piano* by Hansol Jung and *Wondrous Strange* by Martyna Majok, Meg Miroshnik, Jiehae Park and Jen Silverman.

revisit it as an adult. That feeling trips you up, the way the wires got tangled on the oversize set pieces.

The ruptured illusion made these perceptions even more sharp. A rapid repair effort was happening, but something extraordinary was also happening onstage during the stoppage. There was a sublime awareness of the moment in the moment. This was not how it was supposed to go, to have the calibrated "irruptions of the real," to import Lehmann's term, that Ruhl, Waters and Smart created upstaged by an actual mistake – an even more direct irruption of the real (2006: 100). It's funny how an audience feels vulnerable and as if they have failed when the performance stops like that: it feels like your own mortality too. In Berkeley, three months later, all went smoothly in the final movement, which meant it was interrupted, but on purpose. The third act creates a purposeful mess, but it lacked the mess of the unplanned, especially the flash of irritation from the actors. That second incarnation felt more melancholy than effervescent; but both caught the messy way staging Ruhl's writing scenographically unites presence and absence.

Life/Afterlife/Theatre

With its focus on late-in-life transitions and the theatrical re-playing of childhood, *For Peter Pan on Her 70th Birthday* bends and layers time and space. The worlds or realities of the play go almost fractal because of the age of the characters, the occasion for their gathering and the way that their role-play folds in on itself in the show's overlapped spatiality. Since the play is about aged characters, some of what they do in the action is remember earlier parts of their lives. Memory fabricates the play's spatiotemporal density and creates some of the sense of multiplying realities: there's now and there's all the parts of the past that each of the siblings has distinct, overlapping and sometimes contradictory memories about. But *For Peter Pan* is not primarily a memory play; it is more like *Six Characters in Search of an Author*: it is life trying to mobilize itself through character archetype. Ann's resumption of the role of Peter Pan and the emergence of a children's theatre performance as the family's manifestation of grief make it go fractal. The structure of the play layers life and the afterlife together in an always present and transforming theatre space.

In *For Peter Pan,* all the characters are over fifty-five, though Ann, the once and future Peter Pan of the title, is herself on the cusp of seventy. The occasion of the play is that the siblings gather to hold vigil at their dying father's bedside. The play is divided into movements, like a symphony. Its first movement is a vigil, the second is a wake and the third a waking dream where Ann and her siblings, asleep in their childhood home, are also in the nursery of the Darling children. Ruhl writes that the time of the play is first "sometime in the Clinton era," then "in the land of memory," and finally, "Neverland, which has no time" (Ruhl, 2018: 7). The space of the play supersedes the hospital and house and transforms the theatre into Neverland. Thus, the three simultaneous realities are layered onstage by the scenographic aspects of Ruhl's writing in *For Peter Pan:* daily life, the afterlife and the theatre.

Ruhl layers the afterlife into the same space as life, offering a series of meditations about how after death people might interact with the reality human perception can apprehend day-to-day. In the first movement, Ann and her siblings sit around their father's deathbed (see Figure 7). He is on life support; the beeping of a machine stands in for his life force. George's breath rises and falls. In this space life and the afterlife hover one on top of the other like horizontal layers, not interpenetrated, but extremely close. The supine body still houses George's life, but the horizon of the afterlife lies just beyond.

In the second movement, Ruhl creates a different composition melding life and afterlife. As the siblings have an "Irish wake" in the dining room of their childhood home, they drink and carouse, debate and remember their father's

Figure 7 The Siblings at the bed side. David Chandler, Ron Crawford, Keith Reddin, Wendy Emert, Kathleen Chalfant and Scott Jacek in *For Peter Pan* at Actors Theatre of Louisville. Photo by Bill Brymer

life. As they do so, the actor who played their father, who had been lying under a thin sheet in the hospital bed in the first movement, walks through the space and interacts with props and set pieces. Along with him comes a dog, the family's old pet. George's presence on stage is not spectral or floating. It is earthy and comic: he goes to the bathroom, he eats, he knocks things over. Ruhl's stage directions read "*He is an ordinary ghost. He has returned home and is going about his business*"(40). He is an "ordinary" ghost going about his business, not Hamlet's father or Banquo or even Jacob Marley with a message for the living. Is an ordinary ghost the opposite of a theatrical ghost?

Ruhl uses the word ghost, but her presentation of the afterlife defies ideas about haunting and immateriality. George's adult children do not perceive him, though the minute he arrives the siblings' memories do turn to how they bought the casket for their mother when she died. As if in counterpoint, George gets up to use the toilet when the siblings get morbid about their fear of long, dark entombments. He flushes the toilet when he is done, which causes the group to comment on how the toilet is always running, and two of the brothers go and fix it. This contrast of the still too human need to defecate and the discussion of Catholicism and burial is both funny and poignant, the aged children both laughing and crying in the dining room pictured in Figure 8.

Later, the siblings' discussion of prayer leads Michael to joke "Dad – if you're here with us, give us a sign." In the silence that follows, George knocks over the Chex mix bowl. "That was creepy" Michael comments, and,

Figure 8 The Siblings at the old family home. Wendy Emert, Keith Reddin, David Chandler, Kathleen Chalfant and Scott Jacek in *For Peter Pan* at Actors Theatre of Louisville. Photo by Bill Brymer

unsettled, he admits his fear of death. Michael is the one to conjure the memory of the family dog, Capp: that is when George returns with the dog, who eats the spilled Chex mix, though the siblings do not notice the assist with the clean-up (52–4). This sequence of prosaic action from the ghost and spiritual conversation among the adult children layers the mundane and the cosmic.

The last thing George does in his ghostly form is mix himself a glass of Metamucil – this is a ghost highly concerned with his bowel functions – and drink it while his children discuss whether God, communion and Santa are metaphors. Ann muses that all myths and religions are most useful as metaphors: "It's funny I think I believe in Tinkerbell more than I do in the afterlife," she says. But Michael declares "a good Catholic doesn't think God is a metaphor. Communion is not supposed to be a metaphor. When the little bell rings it's real." "Like Tinkerbell," says Ann, though she doesn't seem to hear how when George stirs his Metamucil into the glass the spoon makes the glass ring like a bell (60–1). With this reference to the ringing of bells, and an actual ringing, the conversation moves from metaphor to transubstantiation as well as from Catholicism to *Peter Pan*. The bell in the Catholic liturgy links to the way that in children's theatre productions of *Peter Pan* Tinkerbell is sometimes represented by a ringing bell: Tinkerbell uses pixie dust to help Peter and the Darling children fly. Children in the audience are often at that point asked to clap their hands and believe that Pan and the children can fly. Later, Ruhl's play replicates a moment where the audience applauds and believes as hard as possible until the special effect kicks in and the actors are lifted into the air for flight.[17]

With sequences like this, Ruhl's scenographic writing presents life and the afterlife as happening in the same space at all times, the same molecules co-present in layered embodiment. The ringing of the bell, the question of belief in transubstantiation, brings around the third layer of Ruhl's spatiotemporal experimentation: the theatre and its vertical theatricality. The theatre can represent things that we cannot perceive but which may be a truth of the universe. Ruhl begins and ends *For Peter Pan* in the theatre, specifically, the theatre where the audience is watching the show. The script directs that the actor playing Ann starts the play and ends the play in a simple, stripped down way, talking to the audience: "Hello, I'll be playing Peter Pan," she says (9). She is already Ann here, but for a moment it is phenomenologically slippery: the audience is not sure whether Kathleen Chalfant is talking as Kathleen

[17] Christopher Durang's famous monologue in his short play *'dentity Crisis* also records how common this aspect of productions of *Peter Pan* was in post war community and children's theatre.

Chalfant or as her character (or a version of Ruhl's mother who once played Peter Pan). She may be all of those, and the prologue holds in suspension a *theatrum mundi*, memories of a very specific theatre in Iowa and the very theatre where the show is now about to begin.

Ann's monologue between movements two and three and the epilogue of the show also happen in this layered, liminal theatre space as well. There are many photos documenting this transitional joint in the play's structure because it is when Ann changes into her Peter Pan costume. She is in the here and now with us in the theatre, she reflects on the family reunion we've just watched and she remembers performing in *Peter Pan*, then movement three begins. Figure 9 shows the oversized scale of the dream nursery in Smart's design for this act, and Chalfant in costume as Pan, proposing to take flight. These design and embodiment choices convey what Ruhl indicates in her script note when she writes, "Movement Three should often feel like full-on children's theater, arms akimbo, with real people hovering underneath their roles in *Peter Pan*" (7). The play's third movement happens in a dreamlike space–time that operates *as if* Ann and her siblings are performing a play and *as if* they themselves are passing over into the afterlife while also being a stylized continuation of the depiction of their life in the days after their father's death as they face being the grown-ups and have bad dreams. Ruhl's scenographic layering builds momentum and combines with

Figure 9 Arms Akimbo. Wendy Emert and Kathleen Chalfant in *For Peter Pan* at Actors Theatre of Louisville. Photo by Bill Brymer

a linguistic and rhythmic playfulness that results in a convergence of life, afterlife and the theatre in the play's third movement.

Pauses and Outbursts

Ruhl indicates in her texts that there should be overlaps in dialogue the way Churchill does, though without using the backslash technique. Instead, she uses long em-dashes to suggest pauses and dovetailing; she gives stage directions that indicate overlapping; she also sets up dialogue in parallel columns on the page to indicate the flow of simultaneous talking. On the page, Ruhl's plays can look disjointed, little fragments of speech, short sentences; sometimes it looks a little like e.e. cummings poetry. Ruhl's dramaturgy takes this type of playfulness with typography as a given. She also employs it as a reflection of the messiness of prosaic speech. The *For Peter Pan* script note describes her use of language in this play as an indication of shared family intimacy: "dialogue sometimes lacks capitalization or punctuation when it seems as though the characters are finishing each other's sentences," she writes. "There is a certain musicality of speech when a family of five is talking" (7). In other words, Ruhl's treatment of dialogue paradoxically employs techniques that could be used to produce anti-naturalistic effects to create a type of realism of daily dialogue.

Ruhl does several further things with games, codes and treatment of the subject matter through language that troubles more comfortable approaches to plot, character and theme. She plays with theatre's expressive elements in this way. The first thing she does is that the script does not name the characters. Instead, the siblings are numbered 1–5. The five children of George correspond to "the five" sons of the Lleweyllyn family for whom JM Barrie wrote *Peter Pan*. The Peter Pan intertext is like a numerical cipher. Ruhl's list of the characters in the front matter specifies that 1 is Ann, 2 is John, 3 is Jim aka James Hook, so he becomes Captain Hook in the third movement. Four is Michael, 5 is Wendy, who, turnabout, is the youngest of the family even though in Barrie's story Wendy is older than her brothers. Yet the main text of the play does not use the character names to indicate who is speaking; it uses the numbers. The characters refer to each other by their names in their dialogue, but reading the script is more difficult than expected because of the numbers: it's more like an open text experience, though, of course Ruhl has not gone so far as to deny all character designation or leave the text to be broken up by actor and director, as she does for the chorus in her version of *Orlando*.

The most delicate aspect of Ruhl's language in *For Peter Pan* is how it conveys the characters' difficulty putting into words their understanding of death, whatever they feel about life and the afterlife. In performance, the actors often played the moment of not having the right words, of stumbling to construct a sentence. Words often fail the characters, so they make references instead. This is where the allusive qualities of Ruhl's intertextual use of *Peter Pan*, in both Barrie and Disney's manifestations, really take flight. Every reference to being orphans (lost boys) or not wanting to be grown up echoes with resonance to *Peter Pan*. During the wake, all the characters talk about when they felt they were truly grown up. Several of them can pinpoint the moment, others, like Ann and Jim, still, don't feel like grown-ups:

> 3:
> Well, if you don't grow up you don't have to die.
> Here's to not growing up, Ann. You and me
> 1:
> Here's to not growing up.
> *3 and 1 clink glasses.*
> 4:
> You can grow up before you die or not grow up
> before you die, but you die either way. (58–9)

It matters that the siblings two most afraid of death are the two who double as Peter Pan and Captain Hook, enemies and star playmates in the role-play of authority and rebellion that is *Peter Pan*. J.M. Barrie's *Peter Pan* is about dealing with loss and so is Ruhl's *For Peter Pan*; the key insight of both texts is that avoiding loss makes it worse. But the instinct is to avoid. Ann says "dying is such a failure" and, in a piece of prose worthy of Barrie's propaganda to recruit soldiers for WWI "our bodies are the enemy and dying is a capitulation, to a foreign shore." With thanks to Hamlet, death may be an undiscovered country, but Ann is perhaps a warrior instead of a traveler. By the third movement, Ann-as-Pan has shifted to the even more jingoistic Barrie-ism "dying will be an awfully big adventure!"[18] The closing movement of Ruhl's structure, however, lifts Ann and her siblings up, takes her into a new encounter with her father and lets her combine her home and Neverland in the theatre, where she can grow up, die and remain eternally young all at the same time.

Flying

Movement three has Ann-as-Pan shake her siblings awake in a nursery, and Smart's design created this dreamscape locale with a verticality that exceeds and distorts the usual proportions of a house. In the course of the movement, the siblings reenact being cast forth into the world to make sense of growing up. The life and death stakes that they explore in this dream state of consciousness are

[18] *See Feldmeyer (2017) on this phrase in Barry's Peter Pan and its theatrical adaptations.*

whimsical but also terrifying, though one by one, each returns to their adult lives.

In the third movement, the siblings recapitulate some of the events usually featured in *Peter Pan* plays and movies, though Ruhl completely leaves aside offensive encounters with the "Indians" of Neverland. The recognizable beats come slightly out of order, but they are there: Pan losing her shadow, Wendy sewing it back on for her; the arrival of Tinkerbell; a duel with Captain Hook; the trip to Neverland; and the injunction to "think happy thoughts." Crucially, Ruhl separates the initial trip to Neverland from the apotheosis into flight. Instead of *flying* to Neverland the first time, in this dream, the siblings have to *walk* there because in their aging bodies they can't seem to launch into flight yet and Tinkerbell hasn't arrived.

When the group first tries to leave for Neverland, the realities of their daily lives interrupt: Ann's foot is acting up due to gout; Michael needs to take his medicine; Wendy has arthritis. They are beset by a type of mourning for time passing: "Oh, we're getting old, aren't we?" asks John. "Are we getting too old to fly?" (78). This interweaving of the play-real of childhood and the interrupting reality of aging is key to the heightened consciousness the show produces. The audience watches the dream, seeing the immortal self and the mortal self reconcile with theatrical conventions: Ann asks for a cane, and the play presents the absurd and wonderful spectacle of five older people in nightgowns and Peter Pan regalia stomping around the stage in a parade. They sing as they march and, like in children's theatre, they make a circle around the stage and then arrive at their new destination.

In production, the nursery walls rotated at this moment to present the Neverland scenery on the other side: a sea, a volcano, a pirate ship. The key consciousness-turning element, of course, comes with the much anticipated flight. Flight in this script turns out to be an image not of *defeating* death but rather *embracing* it, understanding it. Ruhl's dramaturgy produces a moment of recognition about the nature of consciousness for Ann-Pan. The revelation of the dream play is that flying isn't a defiance of death ("I won't grow up!") but rather an expression of what it feels like after death. Ann-who-is-Pan and Captain Hook duel about half way through the third movement of Ruhl's play, and unlike in Barrie or Disney, Hook in fact slays Peter Pan. While Pan lays on the stage floor dying, her siblings crowd around her body and this is how they latch the flying cables onto her. Wendy gets the audience to applaud and cheer, and then, finally, Ann-Pan floats upwards into the air. The second half of the movement focuses on the experience of death, of moving through the universe and of a type of homecoming in familial and theatrical space.

In Ruhl's scenographic writing, this vertical rise, this theatrical flight, provides an experience of consciousness that helps us know death. Ann's siblings call to her while she swims in the air above them: "what is death really like?" "Does consciousness persist after all?" Ann-Pan says this of death: "It was flying! It was wonderful!" (90). As she flies, a projected image of the siblings' childhood home shows on stage. Once they see the family home, everyone wants to fly. Even Jim-who-is-Hook asks to join, a type of redemption. Ann-Pan sprinkles pixie dust on them and they all harness up. In the first production, Wendy flew solo like Ann. The boys all clambered on the oversize bed set piece and it lifted into the air. It was supposed to be a sort of messy and anti-illusionistic flight. The oversize flats and giant nursery bed made even more visual sense as the performers went vertically into the stage's airspace. This is a planned irruption of the real – we know they're not flying; there is no attempt at seamless illusion (Lehmann, 2006: 100).

This was, of course, the moment when the wires got tangled in Louisville. The flats needed to move to form a central window piece. At the stoppage, all the characters were suspended between life and death, in a way, joking with us from a place between dream and reality. When the play resumed, the siblings flew together to their childhood house and looked through its windows. Ruhl's open-ended stage directions about how to achieve flight allow for low tech, no tech or stylized approaches to flying, but the scenographic aspects of her writing suggest that the sense of a lift and theatrical transformation upwards remains affectively necessary. Until the third movement, the production presented a strong horizontal orientation consistent with the spatial layering of life and death Ruhl builds into the hospital room and dining room. The verticality of flight bends the layers, connecting, Bachelard would say, inhabited space and geometric space (1994: 47).

Then, crucially, the siblings' flight ends because they remember they sold the family house after their father died. Time bends and layers again: in the sequencing of the play, while Ann is dreaming they are in the house the night after the wake, just after their father died. In the space–time of the dream, they are also moving forward into the months and weeks after their father's death. The house is sold; they celebrate Ann's seventieth birthday; John and Michael go back to work; Wendy rejoins her husband. One by one the children come down from their flight because they remember their spouses, their children, their pets and the careers they love.

Except Ann. As the movement ends, she continues to fly around as if above her hometown. She sees the Davenport Children's Theatre. When she lands there, she has the conversation with her father described in Section 1. He tells her he is proud of her. They embrace and she watches him walk away.

Spatiotemporally, the play sheds light on how she will let him go fully over to death and how she will go back to life. Death is not an undiscovered country. In this construct, death is an undiscovered parallel universe; or, death is the singularity that allows us to step over into the other reality. Alternately, as Einstein could have it, we are stepping over from one into another all the time, we just don't recognize it, except, perhaps, in the theatre.

Family Drama and Children's Theatre

Like many of Ruhl's plays, *For Peter Pan* is a family romance rendered with high intertextual vibrancy. On the one hand, *For Peter Pan*, more than most of her plays, signals recognizably as an American family drama because of how it presents family dynamics, treating the family as the self-contained microcosm of the world. On the other hand, Ruhl's play is not as much of a *dysfunctional* family drama like classics of the genre that center on intractable struggles and the revelation of a shameful family secret, such as Eugene O'Neill's *Long Day's Journey Into Night* or Sam Shepherd's *The Buried Child*. Dramaturg Madeleine Oldham discusses the problem of genre in a patron email sent during the Berkeley Rep run of *For Peter Pan*, arguing that Ruhl emphasizes functionality more than dysfunction in her depiction of family.[19] This may be both an expression of philosophy on Ruhl's part and – because she is writing about her own family, importing and transforming real behaviors – a projection and desired reinvention through intertextual adaptation as she considers consciousness and death.

Next, Ruhl's sleight-of-hand with documentary and verbatim theatre in *For Peter Pan* destabilizes the play's relationship to realism: it provides for the way that "the real" is a postdramatic "coplayer" in the show, an irruption that disrupts its fictive frame (Lehmann, 2006: 100). The play uses ethnography and biography of Ruhl's maternal family. Ruhl gives the character Ann some of her mother's specific life experiences. The second movement uses dialogue from interviews Ruhl recorded with her extended Kehoe family, her mother's siblings. This grounding in Ruhl's family history, the semi-verbatim use of recorded dialogue and Ruhl's description that "movements One and Two should feel almost unperformed" asserts a claim on a type of postdramatic troubling of the fictive aspects of dramatic representation (7). Additionally, in the script, Ruhl provides pictures of her mother playing Peter Pan in the 1950s and she includes a picture of the Kehoe family house in Iowa and indicates that it should

[19] Madeline Oldham shared observations about American family drama and Ruhl's revision of it in an email to Berkeley Repertory Theatre subscribers and ticket holders who attended *For Peter Pan* in June of 2016. I attended the show there on June 7, 2016.

be used as a projection in the third movement. She asks that her grandparents' house should be the house Ann and her siblings see during their flight. The real Kehoe home, Ruhl's mother's home, is meant to irrupt into the space and change the course of the Peter Pan play, on both levels.

These biographical and documentary precisions help explain how the play can be a family drama focused on the ghost of a father which is also a birthday gift to her mother. Given this, Ruhl's dramaturgy reorients family drama with feminist and postmodern metaphysical energies, emphasizing transformation instead of trauma, acknowledging the loss of fathers (Ruhl's own, and her grandfather), but also honoring how a mother's identity can model perseverance and reinvention in life.

As part of this feminist and metaphysical reworking of family drama, Ruhl also activates children's theatre as both a set of conventions and a way of thinking about the relationship of the real and the performed. As a mode, children's theatre often knowingly and playfully moves back and forth between inviting the audience to join the pretense through participation and also honoring how totally a young audience may invest in the illusion of the story – think of the way that children's theatre will often have sequences of audience participation, like where a character may hide in the audience and ask the children to misdirect any other character who comes looking for them. But also consider how in children's theatre sometimes when a villain dies onstage they do not come back for curtain call so as not to upset the children's illusion. There is some alchemy in children's theatre, where an enlarged view of the world reciprocally opens up the experience of the self as both real and pretend. When Ann returns to the Davenport Children's Theatre after her flight, she plays out the last scene with her father with the subdued voice and physicality of the grown up she is and must be. In the epilogue, though, she throws some more pixie dust and makes her fantastical exit. The scenographic aspects of Ruhl's writing put the audience in the same real-pretend space with her and also allows the final disappearing act.

5 Form and Tradition

The paradox is that dramatic forms, even as they participate in long traditions, are in a constant state of renovation and innovation. As Liz Tomlin asserts, reclaiming playwriting as part of postdramatic developments in practice, "the dramatic form itself has continuously questioned its own predicates, with a self-reflexivity that has enabled it to dismember the classical dramatic apparatus piece by piece, shape-shifting into the absences that are left almost imperceptibly to form new structures that can accommodate the philosophical questions of the time." The project of this Element has been to use the critical concept of space to open up analysis of contemporary plays as part of reclaiming their phenomenological, philosophical and imagistic vitality. The scenographic nature of contemporary playwriting is part of how text-based theatre also works in a "third register," in Tomlin's terms, that is "neither dramatic/logocentric nor postdramatic, fragmentary 'performance'" (2013: viii).

This conclusion briefly revisits three sets of insights the analysis has developed about the way that space and spatiality constitute important concepts for understanding the combination of text, visuality, staging and embodiment in contemporary playwriting. The first group of ideas has to do with the way that encounters between text and performance communicate spatially both on the page and on the stage. The phenomenological and spatial dimensions of text-based theatre, its scenographic aspects, call into question what writing can do, or what artists can do with writing, as part of creating theatre. The second set of ideas turns on the way that the expressive elements of theatre are multisensory, which positions playwriting as part of a continuum of spatial acts in theatre. Visual dramaturgy as a concept is appealing to describe the structural underpinning of postdramatic plays, but does not go as far as concepts of space do when thinking about re-orderings of theatre's multisensory elements, even in text-based theatre. The third set of ideas concern how the phenomenological and spatiotemporal dimensions contemporary plays have taken on increased importance as the text-based and performance-based traditions combine, yet these aspects of theatre have fewer critical tools to address them. The scenographic aspects of contemporary playwriting deepen and expand the possibilities of dramatic form and how it addresses the world-creating power of a perceiving, embodied mind; they go beyond metatheatre and invite an exciting, quantum sensibility that maximizes the combination and co-creation of literary beauty and theatrical wonder.

What Can Writing Do?

Considering contemporary trends in play structure and dramaturgical modes, Jacqueline Bolton calls for more "inclusive notions of the status and function of text" and "more nuanced approaches to authorship," noting that what is signaled by the distinction "text-based/non-text-based" theatre is not the "simple presence/absence of a pre-existing script," but instead perceptions about what is considered most important in theatre and whether all power is supposed to defer to "the person of the author" (Bolton, 2011: 91, 119). Sarah Sigal identifies the way writers in collaborative processes may now fill the role of writer as co-creator, writer as company scribe or writer as poet; she notes that there may be multiple writers or that a writer may function in the process as a writer/director, writer/dramaturg or writer/artistic director (2016: 16–7). Meanwhile, in *New Performance/New Writing*, John Freeman productively investigates the way theatre writing has "changed in its form over the last century" and therefore now focuses on the question not of who is writing (authorship) or "what can we write," but rather "what can we do with writing" (2007: 14–5). What we can do with writing is a question that looks toward the text as part of the spatial imaginary of theatre as a form.

Freeman (no relation to me) asks this in order to support his efforts to analyze postmodern and postdramatic performance, by which he means "contemporary work that is sometimes more and often knowingly less than theatre, as it is usually described" (3–4). He is wary about playwrights and plays but wants to recuperate writing. Some of the issues around conceiving the forms of contemporary playwriting have to do with the way that experimental work wants to negate theatre as a form by negating the literary traditions of theatre, even as it is itself theatrical performance. This theatre-but-not-theatre status is an element of what Jarcho describes as heritage from Artaud and selective misreading of Derrida's commentary on writing (2020: 3–4). Freeman pierces through the problem of the literary object versus the embodiment of performance when he wonders if writing is solely textual, contending that "writing for performance does not always result in the creation of words to be spoken" (10), which rings as true for Churchill, Iizuka and Ruhl's stage directions as it does for a performance of Forced Entertainment or Frantic Assembly.

As Churchill's history with the use of the Joint Stock Method and other collaborative developmental processes at the Royal Court suggests, a playwright's compositional work in theatre is just as often embedded in long-term processes and collaborations that are not separate from the processes that generate non-text-based work. Iizuka and Ruhl have similar or parallel experiences of process and generation. As a new writing theatre, the Royal Court is quite interesting in terms of how it both elevates authorship, but also puts playwrights into a context where writing is unleashed in multiple ways, back to the early history with the writers' group using improvisatory games and group experiments to propel the creation of shows. At the Court, the space-making processes of the theatre highly interact with the text, whether through the role of designers like Jocelyn Herbert in establishing the Court's aesthetics or in maximizing or managing the upstairs and downstairs spaces in their incarnations over time. A parallel analysis could be undertaken of Actors Theatre of Louisville and the other key new writing theatres where Iizuka and Ruhl find consistent artistic homes.

The way these aspects of text-creation for theatre-making engage especially directors and designers refutes any implication that text-based theatre is the deadweight of performance forms because of the impossible tension between textual logic and other logics. Overall, it is too simple to position text as the opposite of visuals in theatre or to pinpoint dramatic writing or playwrights themselves as a problem to overcome in contemporary theatre. Playwriting in the last thirty years markedly mobilizes text for a spatial imaginary, participating in the re-ordering of expressive elements of theatre that defines both postdramatic theatre and live art forms that are both consciously more and less than theatre in Freeman's terms.

Still, when performance artists who are not playwrights consider writing, this concern with what can be done (or what cannot be done) with writing is a dominant theme and there is a strong emphasis on how visuality and embodiment work. For instance, a forum about "Writing and Performance" in *Performing Arts Journal* (PAJ) provides examples of the perceived tension between the role of text and the embodiment of performance (Mapp et al., 2012). Contributors to the forum consider how common cross-over between live art and dance techniques are within theatre while also seeking to make distinctions between plays and performance art. The forum starts from this premise:

> The evolution of text in performance takes many forms in the last half century: as dramatic literature, as fragment, as archive, as intertext, as poetry. While contemporary transformations in theatre have moved increasingly away from staging new plays in favor of collage-based work, performance in the visual arts has embraced language as a narrative mode, and dance has become both more theatrical and more text-oriented. (119)

This *PAJ* introduction suggests simultaneous movements where directors and designers are using theatre's expressive elements like dance used to use its elements, while visual arts are becoming like storytelling, and dance is becoming theatre, all while declaring that new play production is decreasing in the twenty-first century. This description errs only in thinking playwrights are not part of the trend and that new play production is decreasing.

While the migration of formal aspects among artistic mediums narrated in *PAJ* is easily observable across dance, theatre and visual arts, it combines with an upsurge in new play production in the United States and UK, rather than a decrease, with many of those new plays combining aspects of text and performance in ever more hybrid, spatial ways. But if the spatiality of contemporary playwriting is a mark of its vitality, its interconnectedness to other movements, why has the distinction between text-based and non-text-based theatre been important in the last thirty years? What seems to be most at issue is the intersection of authorship and authority. Insofar as experimentation in performance is understood to be directly anti-authoritarian, or at least non-hierarchically collaborative, the role of writing as a form of authority and authors as the most important artist in a creative hierarchy is targeted in performance theory. New writing theatres are a locus for theatrical experimentation, but they also focus on supporting playwrights and treating playwriting as the main engine of theatrical production. So, despite many moments of rethinking authorship as part of collaborative creation, an author-primary framing (which positions writers as the "first" or "original" artist of the theatre and other theatre artists as interpreters) continues strongly in conceptions of text-based theatre (Sigal, 2016: 6–11).

Literary managers, dramaturgs, designers and directors can support or challenge author-primary discourse, but it is a very easy discourse to use, even though, as Jarcho points out, all modes of theory and experience tell us that "even when actors and directors think they're following or serving a text, they're actually creating something new" (2020: 113). Still, if one of the goals of experimental art is to challenge a culture's dominant ideology, then an important tactic is to upend word-based logic and dissect how structures of language carry that ideology. Non-text-based theatre starts somewhere other than with *logos*, in order to perhaps loosen the tightly knit together strings of ideology, narrative and language. Analysis attentive to the scenographic aspects of playwriting can reveal the way plays resist older hierarchies of ideology too and acknowledge that theatre writing is attempting to sit right alongside all the perception-reshaping contemporary performance forms.

This Element has drawn examples from Churchill, Iizuka and Ruhl's theatre making to explicate these currents around playwriting and space as playwrights mobilize writing and combine it with other signifying logics. The sections have shown how the interplay of superimposed interiority and exteriority in Churchill's *The Skriker* carries its feminist and ecocritical insights about maternity, sustainability and mental health as much as any plot point; similarly, the experience of simultaneity and intimate immensity in Iizuka's *At The Vanishing Point* refigures whiteness and class status from her distinctly Asian-American perspective; and the layered horizontal and vertical expansions of the hospital, the house and the theatre into the universe in Ruhl's *For Peter Pan on Her 70th Birthday* reveal how she alters community theatre and family drama tropes to valorize both agedness and femininity. Playwrights continue to explore with vigor and openness what can writing do and it is reshaping contemporary performance texts.

Why Does Space Matter to Playwriting?

The introduction suggested that if scenography and visual dramaturgy are related in the way that playwriting is related to dramaturgy, then it may be possible to say that the visual dramaturgy of contemporary writing re-spatializes text as part of theatre. Treating playwriting as a spatial act highlights theatre's multisensory expressive elements and encourages phenomenological engagement with text-based theatre, especially the way new plays bring experimental form and content to more mainstream venues. Space as a concept is both conceptual and concrete, imaginative and practical, so it encourages not only dramaturgical analysis of scenography and action, but also a reading of the whole production apparatus around a show as an event in space and part of a city or nation's larger theatre landscape.

Notably, all three productions considered here fly in the face of the way that in new play production, new writing can be expected to be small – in cast size, in spectacle, in appropriate venue. The premiere of Churchill, Iizuka and Ruhl's work at significant theatrical institutions matters to their experimentation with time and space, and the spatiality of the bigness their productions achieve. At first glance, *The Skriker's* premiere in the Cottesloe in the National Theatre complex most replicates the small/big division in new play production. The Cottesloe (renamed the Dorfman in 2013) was the smallest of the National Theatre's venues until the creation of the Studio in 2015. As a flexible space, the Cottesloe held options for space-transformation that suits a shape-shifting play like *The Skriker*, including traps, a functional fly and backstage space, which is not true of many black box spaces and pub theatres where new plays get done. Pub theatre serves as an important context here, because those small, repurposed spaces often have less than 100 seats, like small studios. In comparison, the Cottesloe's 300 seats hardly seem small. In the United States, mainstage houses often possess only 300–500 seats, and houses with 900 or 1,100 seats (like the Olivier and the Lyttleton) are rare except for spaces used for commercial musicals. At the time of *The Skriker's* opening in NT repertoire, Declan Donnelan's 1992 production of Tony Kushner's two *Angels in America* plays was also showing in the Cottesloe. As a new play, *The Skriker* joined a season which in the rest of the building featured a major revival of *Sweeny Todd* and a rediscovery of the 1920s feminist play *Machinal* as well as the premiere of Alan Bennett's *The Madness of King George*. Soon after it left the repertoire, Peter Brook's *The Man Who* came into the Cottesloe and the National premiered Tom Stoppard's *Arcadia* in the Lyttleton – which also stages parallel worlds in overlapping space–time on stage. Thus, *The Skriker* opened during a period at the National Theater where new plays and old plays alike were being staged with staggering bigness and a sense of spatial possibility.

Vanishing Point and *For Peter Pan* both premiered in the mainstage house of Actors Theatre of Louisville, performing in the Pamela Brown auditorium, a theatre with a proscenium arch and 633 seats, as opposed to the in-the-round Bingham Theatre (318 seats) or the black box Victor Jory space (159 seats). Though *For Peter Pan* was part of the Humana Festival, Ruhl's work has almost exclusively appeared on main seasons at ATL and elsewhere: she spent very little time as a writer appearing in under 100 seat venues. The fit between the needs of *For Peter Pan*, like flying five actors and having a marching band parade through, and the large space gave her play's spatiotemporal constructs the scale required. Iizuka's play also opened in the Pamela Brown in 2015, where two other of her plays have premiered during the Humana Festival. Across her career, Iizuka has been programmed in small studios, found spaces, black boxes, site-specific situations, and second stages as well as mainstages. To program both Ruhl and Iizuka's plays in the theatre's central season made their status as new plays significant on scale with the musicals, the revivals of August Wilson and the reinventions of Shakespeare that dominated the programming.[20] Overall, the experiments with expansion and compression of space and time that these three authors undertake came to realization in sizable theatre auditoria, which allowed the scenography to accommodate their shifts and transformations.

Commentary about contemporary playwriting suggests productions like these, at this scale, cause excitement in UK and US theatre. Playwright Simon Stephens thinks the vividness of twenty-first-century British text-based theatre and the heightened spatial imagination now found in the staging of contemporary plays reflects engagement with German theatre, postdramatic texts and a reordering around the priorities of plot, character and language (Barnett, 2016: 316). Tim Sanford, retired artistic director of Playwrights Horizons, declared "We are in a Golden Age of Playwriting" in his keynote address to 2015 Literary Managers and Dramaturgs of the Americas Conference.[21] Sanford's sense that something big was cresting turned on the range and fearlessness of writing and its sense of "dichotomous dynamism," its overall

[20] Actors Theatre of Louisville's 2014–2015 season featured *Love's Labour's Lost*, *Dracula*, *The Last Five Years*, *Tribes*, *A Christmas Carol* and *The Brothers Size;* the 2015–2016 mainstage season started with August Wilson's *Seven Guitars*, and included *Luna Gale* by Rebecca Gilman and *Peter and the Starcatcher*, an interesting dialogue with Ruhl's play in the Festival. When *For Peter Pan* went to Berkeley Rep, it finished a mainstage season that included *Macbeth*, *Disgraced*, *Treasure Island* and a new musical version of the film *Amelie*.

[21] Sara Freeman, personal notes from Tim Sanford Keynote Address, LMDA 2015 Conference, New York City, Columbia University.

capacity to deal with ambiguity and engage stylistic complexity in a sophisticated performance culture. Critic Helen Shaw thinks that an emerging "theatre of the weird" in the United States is making writing exciting because of how it "twine[s] together things that would normally be diametric opposites" (Shaw, 2016).

Shaw sees a theatre that "stretches out its hands" toward the supernatural and uses realism for non-realist ends because of how it overlaps worlds and bends time and space. She is interested in the way contemporary theatre blurs the distinction between experimental and mainstream art and high and low culture. She greets some of the changing ethos in text-based theatre with skepticism because she thinks it is driven by elite institutions running playwriting degrees and that blunts its subversive potential, but she also reacts to the "astonishing beauty" of the theatrical compositions and the occasions for reflection they provide. In essence, Stephens, Sanford and Shaw are responding to the spatial and phenomenological thrust of contemporary playwriting. Artists and critics responding intuitively to the shifting feel of plays this way provide a testament to what a Bachelardian poetics of space illuminates about text-based theatre.

How Do We Talk about Text-Based Theatre?

As noted in the introduction, the phenomenological and spatiotemporal dimensions of playwriting have taken on increased importance as what Fuchs calls the text-based and performance-based traditions of theatre intertwine (2019: 29). Fuchs posits that the text-based tradition and the performance-based tradition "constitute *separate theatre cultures*, either 'drama' in Peter Szondi's sense, or performance theatre in Hans-Thies Lehmann's postdramatic sense" (21). Fuchs describes that these two strands have different "design interests, performance techniques, audiences, and physical theatres" (30). Here, Fuchs references Szondi and Lehmann to name different ideas about the ordering of theatre's expressive elements. Szondi offers a theory of modern drama that seeks to valorize the congruence between form and content in the autonomous dramatic tradition, the alignment of theatre's expressive elements ordered by the text. Lehmann, of course, thinks experimentation with theatre's expressive elements has both exceeded and exploded the dramatic tradition, hence the idea of postdramatic theatre, which may have no need of text.

Complicating the question of critical tools, the way text-based theatre is also written into space makes it worth questioning the use of postdramatic as a categorical or descriptive term. If "postdramatic" is a description of genre, then it makes sense to say that a play cannot have both dramatic and postdramatic elements.[22] But if the notion of the postdramatic is a way of talking about form then, since form is an ordering of expressive elements, it becomes possible to conceive of text-based productions as working with the theatre's expressive elements (words and images, rhythm, mood, color, scale, mimetic and non-mimetic representation, narrative, speaking, movement, patterning) in ways that are part of the postdramatic stage of theatre Lehmann identifies.

Indeed, the search for ways to describe what is happening with theatre's expressive elements carries different nuances and preoccupations depending on the position of the person describing a show and considering what propels and renews theatre. Fuchs, Jarcho, Tomlin and others reclaim the critical tools of performance studies and postdramatic theory to diagnose how text-based theatre participates in the reordering of expressive elements, but also still creates plays (as opposed to some other performance formation). Sigal captures through dramaturgical documentation how the role of writers and writing in contemporary experimental theatre is not negated – rather the conscious copying and modification of existing playwriting practices are a fertile part of theatre generation and innovation (18). Playwriting teacher Paul Castagno comes at it from another angle: he identifies a new style in theatre, positioning a combination of "dramatic and theatrical poetics" as the emerging dominant form of playwriting in his manual *New Playwrighting Strategies: Language and Media in the 21st Century.* Castagno notes an upsurge in plays which "mark contemporary playwrights' unease with traditional narrative through a conflation of dramaturgies and source materials" and "blend the traditional and new poetics, the dramatic and the theatrical" (2011: 1, 5). He wants to teach other writers to be capable of working formally in the "new" style.

It is interesting to watch the slippage of terms across these different modes of analysis, whether it is scholarly criticism or playwriting instruction. Castagno's traditional and new poetics (the dramatic and theatrical) correspond to Fuchs's "two traditions," which she defines with specific reference to Szondi's theories. Yet Castagno uses the term "dialogic" in exactly the opposite way Szondi does in relation to dramatic writing: in the "text-based tradition" Fuchs describes via Szondi, dialogic means that all of the storytelling must happen through the action, that is, it must be absolutely dramatic and never narrative, with dialogue as the only type of linguistic tool a writer has for creating the fiction and conveying the action. Castagno, meanwhile, uses dialogic to mean language-driven and polyphonic in structure rather than character or plot-driven and unified in structure.

[22] My thanks to Peter Campbell for his conversations with me about this manuscript and for prompting ideas in this paragraph in particular.

Castagno's invocation of "dialogic" seems instead to call on a Bahktinian frame about polyvocality, exchange between listeners and receivers, the blending of poetics and the intersection of multiple registers or modes of performance in a single construct. In the performance-based tradition on its own, not combined into "new" playwriting or a Fuchsian hybrid, the role of text and of storytelling or fiction-creation might be entirely vacated. All of these slippages suggest that the scenographic aspects of contemporary playwriting are an attempt to address what can be framed as the problem of text (Radosavljevic, 2013: 7). Space as a concept with equal applicability to text-based theatre may provide a way out of what can feel like a critical mise-en-abyme about the nature of action, representation, structure, fiction and authorship. Instead we might talk about how the activation of space in text-based theatre marks how contemporary playwrights now understand themselves within an embodied and visual medium, and how the scenographic aspects of contemporary playwriting illuminate the artfulness of theatre traditions.

Conclusion

Theatre studies has needed to better describe the artfulness of contemporary text-based theatre as connected to performance innovation, and must respond to the performance of theatre writing with the same sophisticated lenses scholars and critics have used for live art practices and "performance" writ large since the 1970s. Summaries of plot, character analyses, explications of themes, while foundational, cannot do justice to the conceptual and concrete phenomenological impact of theatre. Each of the plays in this study presents a spatiotemporal construct that sheds light on how myths, geography and family history make and transform human consciousness and how that impacts perception through performance: *The Skriker* works with the superimposition of interior and exterior; *At the Vanishing Point* employs the simultaneity of things before and after, in front of and behind each other; *For Peter Pan* layers horizons and vertical lifts, life and afterlife continuous and intersecting. Collaborative practices, design innovations and new theories of space and spatiality have not eradicated text in theatre and performance; instead, contemporary playwriting has made text as necessary and vibrant as any other element of performance in the twenty-first century.

References

Al-Shamma, J. (2011). *Sarah Ruhl: A Critical Study of the Plays*. London: McFarland.

Arntzen, K. O. (1991). A Visual Kind of Dramaturgy: Project Theatre in Scandinavia. In C. Schumacher and D. Fogg, eds., *Small Is Beautiful 1990: Small Countries Theatre Conference*. Glasgow: IFTR Theatre Studies, pp. 43–8.

Aronson, A. (2005). *Looking into the Abyss: Essays on Scenography*. Ann Arbor: University of Michigan Press.

Bachelard, G. (1994). *The Poetics of Space*. Translated by M. Jolas. Boston: Beacon Press.

Barnett, D. (2016). This Is Why I Am Really Excited about British Theatre in the Next Five Years: David Barnett in Conversation with Simon Stephens. *Contemporary Theatre Review* 26(3), 311–18.

Bolton, J. (2011). *Demarcating Dramaturgy: Mapping Theory onto Practice*. Dissertation. University of Leeds.

Brantley, B. (1996). A Land of Fairy Tales Creepily Come True. Rev. of *The Skriker*. *The New York Times*, 16 May, C15. www.nytimes.com/1996/05/16/theater/theater-review-a-land-of-fairy-tales-creepily-come-true.html

Caplan, B. (1994). The Duel in the Crone. Rev. of *The Skriker*. *New Statesman and Society* 7(288), 43–4.

Castagno, P. (2011). *New Playwriting Strategies: Language and Media in the 21st Century*. London: Routledge.

Churchill, C. (1998). *Plays Three*. London: Nick Hern Books.

Cummings, S. T. (2022). *The Theatre of Les Waters: More Like the Weather*. New York: Routledge.

De Certeau, M. (1984). *The Practice of Everyday Life*. Translated by S. Randall. Berkeley: University of California Press.

Devin, L. (1997). Conceiving the Forms: Play Analysis for Production Dramaturgy. In G. Proehl, S. Jonas and M. Lupu, eds., *Dramaturgy and American Theatre: A Sourcebook*. New York: Harcourt Brace, pp. 209–19.

Durham, L. A. (2013). *Women's Voices on American Stages in the Early Twenty-first Century: Sarah Ruhl and Her Contemporaries*. New York: Palgrave Macmillan.

Feldmeyer, L. F. (2017). Preparing Boys for War: J. M. Barrie's Peter Pan Enlists in World War I's "Great Adventure." *Theatre History Studies* 36, 57–74.

Foucault, M. (1986). *Of Other Spaces*. Translated by J. Miskowiec. Diacritics Vol. 16, pp. 22–27.

Freeman, J. (2007). *New Performance/New Writing*. London: Palgrave Macmillan.

Fuchs, E. (2019). Drama: The Szondi Connection. In M. S. Boyle, M. Cornish and B. Woolf, eds., *Post Dramatic Theatre and Form*. London: Methuen, pp. 20–30.

Gobert, R. D. (2014). *The Theatre of Caryl Churchill*. London: Bloomsbury.

Iizuka, N. (2005). *At the Vanishing Point*. In T. Palmer and A. Hansel, eds., *Humana Festival 2004: The Complete Plays*. Hanover, NH: Smith and Kraus, pp. 277–307.

Iizuka, N. (2015). *At the Vanishing Point*. Typescript shared with author by ATL Literary Office.

Jarcho, J. (2020). *Writing and the Modern Stage: Theatre Beyond Drama*. London: Cambridge University Press.

Kaye, D. and LeBrecht, J. (2015). *Sound and Music for the Theatre: The Art and Technique of Design*. London: Routledge.

Kiely, D. (2016). *How to Read a Play: Script Analysis for Directors*. London: Routledge.

Kiely, D. (2020). *How to Rehearse a Play: A Practical Guide for Directors*. London: Routledge.

Kipp, L. M. (2018). "What Is This Place … ?": Howard Barker's Spatial Scenography. *Journal of Contemporary Drama in English* 6(2), 249–64.

Knopf, R. and Listengarten, J., eds. (2011). *Theater of the Avant-Garde 1950–2000: A Critical Anthology*. New Haven: Yale University Press.

Krech, L. (2010). Towards an Understanding of Visual Dramaturgy. Blog, 19 April. http://lucaskrech.com/blog/index.php/2010/04/19/towards-an-understanding-of-visual-dramaturgy/.

Lee, E. K. (2006). *A History of Asian-American Theatre*. Cambridge: Cambridge University Press.

Lefebvre, H. (1991). *The Production of Space*. Translated by D. Nicholson-Smith. Oxford: Blackwell Publishing.

Lehmann, H. T. (2006). *Postdramatic Theatre*. Translated by K. Jurs-Münby. London: Routledge.

López, T. A. (2016). The 1980s: Latina/o Literature during the "Decade of the Hispanic." In J. M. González, ed., *The Cambridge Companion to Latina/o American Literature*. New York: Cambridge University Press, pp. 91–110.

London, T., Pesner, B. and Giroud Voss, Z. (2009). *Outrageous Fortune: The Life and Times of the New American Play*. New York: Theatre Development Fund.

Mapp, J., Skipitares, T., Jesurun, J., et al. (2012). Forum on Writing and Performance. *PAJ: A Journal of Performance and Art* 34(1), 119–40.

Marranca, B. (1977). *Theatre of Images: Robert Wilson, Richard Foreman, Lee Breuer*. New York: Drama Book Specialists.

Massey, D. (1994). *Space, Place, and Gender*. Minneapolis: University of Minnesota Press.

McKinney, J. and Butterworth, P. (2009). *The Cambridge Introduction to Scenography*. Cambridge: Cambridge University Press.

McMullen, A. (2012). Samuel Beckett's Scenographic Collaboration with Jocelyn Herbert. *Degrés: Revues de Synthèse à Orientation Sémiotique* 149–150, 1–17.

Megson, C. (2013). "And I Was Struck Still by Time": Contemporary British Theatre and the Metaphysical Imagination. In V. Angelaki, ed., *Contemporary British Theatre: Breaking New Ground*. London: Palgrave Macmillan, pp. 32–56.

Metzger, S. (2011). *At the Vanishing Point*: Theater and Asian/American Critique. *American Quarterly* 63(2), 277–300.

Miyagawa, C. (1997). Brave, Bold, and Poetic: The New Generation of Asian American Women Playwrights. In J. Peterson and S. Bennett, eds., *Women Playwrights of Diversity: A Bio-Bibliographic Sourcebook*. Westport: Greenwood Press, pp. 13–16.

O'Hara, R. (2011). Conversation with Christina Anderson about *Man in Love*. Steppenwolf Theatre Blog. www.steppenwolf.org/articles/man-in-love-playwright-and-director-in-conversation/.

Pavis, P. (2013). *Contemporary Mise-en-Scène: Staging Theatre Today*. Translated by J. Anderson. London: Routledge.

Pearce, W., Green-Rogers, M. K., Gleason, C. and Maxwell, J. (2018). Visual Dramaturgy: Problem Solver or Problem Maker in Contemporary Performance Creation. *Theatre/Practice* 7, 1–44. www.theatrepractice.us/volume7.html.

Poll, M. (2018). *Robert LePage's Sceneographic Dramaturgy: The Aesthetic Signature at Work*. New York: Palgrave Macmillan.

Quigley, K. (2020). *Performing the Unstageable: Success, Imagination, Failure*. London: Methuen.

Radosavljevic, D. (2013). *Theatre Making: The Interplay between Text and Performance in the 21st Century*. New York: Palgrave.

Reagan, A. (2017). Maria Irene Fornes, World Builder. *American Theatre*, 5 July. www.americantheatre.org/2017/07/05/maria-irene-fornes-world-builder/.

Rebellato, D. (2013). Exit the Author. In V. Angelaki, ed., *Contemporary British Theatre: Breaking New Ground*. London: Palgrave Macmillan, pp. 9–31.

Remshardt, R. (1995). Rev. of *The Skriker*. *Theatre Journal* 47(1), 121–3.

Rosen, M. (2015). ATL's *Vanishing Point*: Poetic Script, Magical Acting. *Leo Weekly*, 4 February. www.leoweekly.com/2015/02/theater-atls-vanishing-point-poetic-script-magical-acting/.

Ruhl, S. (2001). Six Small Thoughts on Fornes, the Problem of Intention, and Willfulness. *Theatre Topics* 11(2), 187–204.

Ruhl, S. (2018). *For Peter Pan on Her 70th Birthday*. New York: Theatre Communications Group.

Ruhl, S. (2019). On Caryl Churchill. People's *Light* Theatre Blog. www.peopleslight.org/blog/2019/sarah-ruhl-on-caryl-churchill/.

Saivetz, D. (2000). *An Event in Space: Joanne Akalitis in Rehearsal*. New York: Smith and Kraus.

Shaw, H. (2016). The State of the Play: A Critic Addresses the Theatre Nation. *American Theatre* 33(8), 30–33. www.americantheatre.org/2016/09/21/the-state-of-the-play-a-critic-addresses-the-theatre-nation/.

Sierz, A. (2008). Reality Sucks: The Slump in British New Writing. *PAJ: A Journal of Performance and Art* 30(2), 102–7.

Sierz, A. (2011). *Rewriting the Nation: British Theatre Today*. London: Bloomsbury Methuen.

Sigal, S. (2016). *Writing in Collaborative Theatre-Making*. London: Palgrave MacMillan.

Sugiera, M. (2004). Beyond Drama: Writing for Post Dramatic Theatre. *Theatre Research International* 29(1), 16–28.

Svich, C. (2006). US Polyglot Latino Theatre and Its Link to the Americas. *Contemporary Theatre Review* 16(2), 189–97.

Svich, C. and Marrero, M. T. (2000). *Out of the Fringe: Contemporary Latina/Latino Theatre and Performance*. New York: Theatre Communications Group.

Tomlin, L. (2013). Dramatic Developments. In V. Angelaki, ed., *Contemporary British Theatre: Breaking New Ground*. London: Palgrave Macmillan, pp. viii–xxvi.

Tompkins, J. (2014). *Theatre's Heterotopias: Performance and the Cultural Politics of Space*. London: Palgrave MacMillan.

Tuan, Y. (1977). *Space and Place: The Perspective of Experience*. Minneapolis: University of Minnesota Press.

Ullom, J. (2008). *The Humana Festival: The History of New Plays at Actors Theatre of Louisville*. Carbondale: Southern Illinois University Press.

Vanden Heuvel, M. (1991). *Performing Drama/Dramatizing Performance: Alternative Theatre and the Dramatic Text.* Ann Arbor: University of Michigan Press.

Veltman, C. (2007). Les Waters: Explorer with an Ear. *American Theatre*, 24(10), 42–7.

Wren, C. (2002). Navigating Alien Worlds. *American Theatre* 19(2), 32.

Zeigler, T. (2015). ATL Revisits Butchertown in Revival of *At the Vanishing Point. Broadway World*, 10 February. www.broadwayworld.com/louisville/article/BWW-Reviews-ATL-Revisits-Butchertown-in-Revival-of-AT-THE-VANISHING-POINT-20150210.

Acknowledgments

All my thanks to Geoff and Mike who always believed in me; to the University of Puget Sound who consistently funded my trips to see shows; and for my children and my mother.

About the Author

Sara Freeman is Professor of Theatre Arts at the University of Puget Sound. She researches contemporary playwriting and alternative, political and feminist theatre. She is a series editor for Methuen's Student Editions of Drama, associate editor of the *Encyclopedia of Modern Theatre* and past editor of *Theatre History Studies*.

Cambridge Elements

Contemporary Performance Texts

About the Series

Contemporary Performance Texts responds to the evolution of the form, role and meaning of text in theatre and performance in the late twentieth and twenty-first centuries, by publishing Elements that explore the generation of text for performance, its uses in performance, and its varied modes of reception and documentation.

Cambridge Elements

Contemporary Performance Texts

Elements in the Series

Playwriting, Dramaturgy and Space
Sara Freeman

A full series listing is available at: www.cambridge.org/ECTX.

Printed in the USA
CPSIA information can be obtained
at www.ICGtesting.com
CBHW061143091024
15595CB00006B/366

9 781009 370226